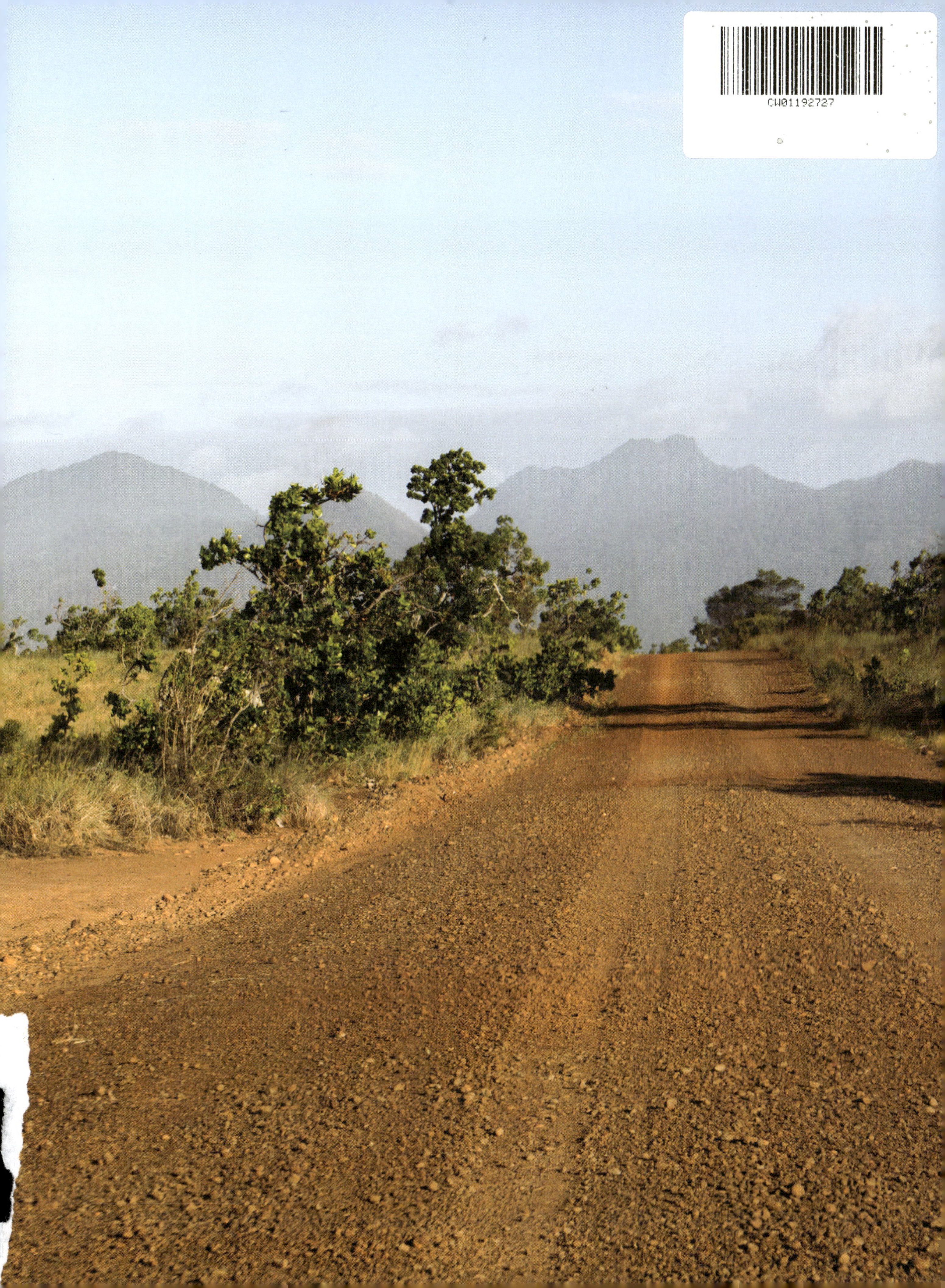

# Guyana at 50

## Reflection, Celebration and Inspiration

Edited by Arif Ali

*Commemorating the Golden Jubilee
Anniversary of Independence, 1966 to 2016*

**HANSIB**

First published in Great Britain by Hansib Publications in 2016

Hansib Publications Limited
P.O. Box 226, Hertford, SG14 3WY

info@hansibpublications.com
www.hansibpublications.com

Copyright © Hansib Publications Ltd, 2016

Images copyright © Individually-credited photographers/photographic sources (in alphabetical order): Robert Arrington (RA), Ian Brierley (IB), Carl Brown (CB), Chris Collins (CC), Dirk Ercken (DE), Robert J. Fernandes (RJF), FotoNatura (FN), Guyana Chronicle (GC), Guyana Tourism Authority (GTA), Dwayne Hackett (DH), L. Haynes (LH), Roger Hinds (RH), T. Horsley (TH), Iwokrama International Centre (IIC), Kurt Jordan (KJ), Kevin Loughlin (KL), Ministry of Education/Department of Culture, Youth & Sport (MED), Pete Oxford (PO), Kirk Smock (KS), A. Snyder (AS), R. Thomas (RT), Donald Webber (DW).

Front endpaper: Rupununi; back endpaper: Rainforest canopy. Photos by Ian Brierley

ISBN 978-1-910553-57-2

A CIP catalogue record for this book
is available from the British Library

All rights reserved.
Without limiting the rights under copyright reserved above, no part of this publication may be reproduced, stored in or introduced into a retrieval system, or transmitted, in any form or by any means (electronic, mechanical, photocopying, recording or otherwise), without the prior written permission of both the copyright owner and the publisher of this book.

Produced by Hansib Publications Limited
United Kingdom

# *Foreword*

A number of Caribbean nations have celebrated, or are about to celebrate, the 50th anniversary of their independence from Britain and each would make claims for specific and distinct features that set them above each other. Guyana is no different, but what distinguishes the Republic of Guyana above many independent and sovereign states are its specific historic, physical, cultural and political configurations that define its peoples, its landscape and drivers that propel it to the future.

And so preparing the text for this publication was a journey of discovery; taking me on several pathways that, as a returning native of the country, I found illuminating, fascinating and challenging.

It is often taken for granted that Guyana is a multicultural and pluralistic society with all its peoples contributing to the forging of the nation out of an untamed land; forging a resilience and fortitude that typifies the Guyanese citizen, here and in the Diaspora. That the country's unique geographic positioning and its socio-political heritage put it at the gateway of South America and the Caribbean, straddling both like the proverbial colossus. That the dream of nationhood, predicated on the republican ideal of egalitarianism, when challenged by the reality of the prevailing geopolitical situation, saw an outpouring of determination – personal and political – and innovative and creative coping strategies that are truly unique to Guyana. I hope that the following pages are unchallenged testimonies of this.

We have chronicled the complexity of this Guyanese landscape, seen from the eyes of its citizens of all political persuasions, ages and geographical locations. From different and differing communities. From its Diaspora. From the nation's current leaders.

There is clearly much to celebrate and much to reflect, and it is hoped that this publication will be the impetus to celebrate this historic milestone and, at the same time, provide the platform for reflection.

**Arif Ali**
**Editor**

# *Acknowledgements*

Sincere thanks are due to the following for their help, support and contribution towards the publication of *Guyana at 50: Reflection, Celebration and Inspiration*.

First of all, to President David A. Granger and the Government of Guyana; Minister Nicolette Henry, who was 'hands-on' throughout the project; and Dr James Rose, without whose support the task of producing the book within such a limited time would have been impossible.

To the members of staff in the Ministry of the President, Yvonne Raghoo, Shalina Singh, and to the staff in Minister Henry's office, Cindy Stewart, Yvonne Cole and Anita George among others.

For their sterling work, our colleagues in the UK, Hansib's Managing Director, Kash Ali, Associate Editor, Ansel Wong, Ella Barnes and Alan Cross; our colleagues in Guyana, coordinating editors / researchers, Russel Lancaster and Petamber Persaud, and to Mark Cumberbatch and Terrance Moore. To the other members of our UK team, Shareef Ali and Richard Painter. To Tota Mangar for meeting our last-minute deadlines. Our printers, Jellyfish Solutions and their staff, Samantha Dewey, Ken Walker and Lisa Regan. The translators, Intonation Limited, Scott Kendall, Titiana Poliakova, and Rachael Cox among others.

And a special thank you to the contributors

Writers (in alphabetical order): Prof Frank Birbalsingh, Damian Fernandes, Terrence Fletcher, Dane Gobin, David A. Granger, Christobel Hughes, Christopher A. Johnson, Marjorie Kirkpatrick, Russel Lancaster, Tota C. Mangar, Ian McDonald, Mary Noel Menezes, Dr Paloma Mohamed Martin, Jasmaine Payne, Merlin O. Persaud, Petamber Persaud, Desmond Roberts, Donald Sinclair, Kirk Smock, Mosa Telford, Ansel Wong

Photographers/Photographic Sources (in alphabetical order): Robert Arrington, Ian Brierley, Carl Brown, Chris Collins, Dirk Ercken, Robert J. Fernandes, FotoNatura, Guyana Chronicle, Guyana Tourism Authority, Dwayne Hackett, L. Haynes, Roger Hinds, T. Horsley, Iwokrama International Centre, Kurt Jordan, Kevin Loughlin, Ministry of Education/Department of Culture, Youth & Sport, Pete Oxford, Kirk Smock, A. Snyder, R. Thomas, Donald Webber

And, in no particular order, thanks to Sir Shridath Ramphal, Ian McDonald, Minister Valerie Garrido-Lowe, Donald Sinclair (Director General, Ministry of Tourism), Permanent Secretary Alfred King, Khalid Hassan, Fazeel Feroze, Elisabeth Harper, Indranauth Haralsingh (Director, Guyana Tourism Authority), Lloyd Austin (Austin's Book Services), Paloma Mohamed Martin, Guyana Chronicle website, Nigel Williams (Editor-in-Chief, Guyana Chronicle), Gariann Daw (Librarian, Guyana Chronicle), Akash Persaud (Senior Graphics/Advertising Department, Guyana Chronicle), Calvin Marks (Supervisor/Advertising Department, Guyana Chronicle), Aubrey Harricharran (Library, Guyana Chronicle), Nickeisha Bristol (Library, Guyana Chronicle), Government Information Agency (GINA), Lokeraj Rupnarain (IT Administrator, Guyana Tourism Authority), Quincy Hinds, Mary McDonald, Hessaun Nandalal, Relindor Kanhai, Chaitnarine Persaud, Karen Bacchus-Hinds and Julet Robertson of New Era Books, Patrick Zephyr (Guyana Small Business Association), Dolly Rahaman, Dorothy Wong, Carlene Cross, Ayinde Burgess, Wayne Gregory, Rema Diallo, Luke Daniels, Suilin Wong, Faiyaz Alli, Patsy Fagan, Zed Mirza, Godfrey Phil, Cyntac Wong, John Mair, Steve Connolly, Desmond Mohamed, Dr Vibert Cambridge, Raquel Thomas-Caesar, Shara Seelall (Tourism, Marketing & PR Coordinator, Iwokrama International Centre), Farouk Nandah, Francis Williams-Smith, Khadifa Wong, Naseem Nasir and Denis Case (Guyana Lands and Surveys Commission), Carla Browne, Explore Guyana Magazine, Guyana Entertainment Magazine (GEM), Allyson Stoll, Jennifer Wishart, the National Library, Gomatie Gangadin (Ministry of the Presidency), Mokesh Daby (CEO/President, Grand Coastal Hotel), Maylene Stephen (Deputy Regional Executive Officer, Region 10), A. Waddell (Information Officer, Regional Democratic Council, Region 4), Susan Isaacs (General Manager, Pegasus Hotel Guyana), Beverley Alert (GINA), Annette Arjoon-Martins (Air Services Limited), Guyana Lands and Surveys Commission, Iwokrama International Centre and the management and staff at the Pegasus Hotel Guyana for going beyond the call of duty to ensure that we were well taken care of.

Apologies and thank you to those contributors whose work we were unable to use and to those whom I may have inadvertently forgotten to mention.

And finally, to Pamela Mary for caring so much.

**Arif Ali**
**April 2016**

# Contents

| | |
|---|---|
| A Message from the President of Guyana, David Granger | 7 |
| Welcome to *Guyana at 50* by Minister Nicolette Henry | 9 |
| Ministers of Government | 10 |
| Map of Guyana | 12 |
| Guyana Facts & Figures | 13 |
| National Anthem of Guyana (Music sheet) | 15 |
| The Song of Guyana's Children (Music sheet) | 16 |
| National symbols of Guyana | 17 |
| Administrative Map of Guyana | 18 |
| Significant events in the history of Guyana | 19 |
| Prime Ministers & Presidents since 1966 | 19 |
| A time for reflection, celebration and inspiration | 21 |
| The long road to Independence | 35 |
| A brief history of Guyana | 40 |
| Our foremost political leaders and the nation | 47 |
| A land of many peoples | 51 |
| So much to see, so much to do | 71 |
| Georgetown in Pictures | 90 |
| Festivals, rituals and holidays | 116 |
| "... If but the wind blows, all her beauty wakes..." | 124 |
| A diverse musical heritage | 130 |
| Cooking Guyanese style | 135 |
| Sport & Pastimes (in pictures) | 140 |
| Distinctively Guyanese or uniquely Guyanese | 149 |
| What's trending in Guyana? | 151 |
| World recognition for Guyana's arts industry | 152 |
| Guyanese literature | 154 |
| A wealth of natural treasures | 157 |
| A rewarding birdwatching experience | 161 |
| Iwokrama – A model for the world | 163 |
| Fifty years of tourism – Guyana's golden opportunity | 173 |
| River and water lores | 181 |
| Painting the wind – A personal reflection | 184 |
| Roads and trails | 186 |
| Guyana from Above (in pictures) | 188 |
| Why invest in Guyana? | 222 |
| Agriculture | 227 |
| Caring for the nation's health and well-being | 234 |
| Spreading the news | 236 |
| The Guyanese Diaspora | 238 |
| Portuguese (Brazilian) language synopsis | 240 |
| Spanish language synopsis | 242 |
| Hindi language synopsis | 244 |
| Chinese (Mandarin) language synopsis | 246 |

Republic Day flag-raising ceremony
on 23 February 2016 / MED

# *A Message from the President of Guyana*

## GUYANA'S FIFTIETH ANNIVERSARY OF INDEPENDENCE

Guyana gained its Independence on 26th May 1966. The celebration of our fiftieth anniversary as an independent nation is truly momentous and joyous.

The observance of this Golden Jubilee is an opportunity to meditate on the lessons of our experiences of nationhood, to celebrate our achievements, to contemplate the destiny of future generations, to continue our mission and to create a good life for all of our people.

This book catalogues some of Guyana's main economic and social achievements. It chronicles the history of its peoples, religions, ethnicities and cultures while recognising their cohesiveness and commonalities.

Guyana's fiftieth anniversary is an opportunity to display the breathtaking beauty of our country. The pages of this book portray, also, our luxuriant natural patrimony. Its depiction of our rare flora and fauna reminds the world that Guyana is the biggest, most beautiful and most bountiful nation in the entire Commonwealth Caribbean.

This commemorative book carries the reader on an exciting journey through the first five decades of our nationhood. It captures, through the use of vivid images and informative text, the events, personalities and entities that have shaped our country's development.

This book is a sample of the offerings of our unique country. We invite you, whether you live in Guyana or are a visitor, to experience, first-hand, the wonders and delights of our great country.

We encourage everyone to come and join us in celebrating our Golden Jubilee!

**David Granger**
**President of the Cooperative Republic of Guyana**

Guyana is known as the land of many waters / IB

# *Welcome to Guyana at 50*

It is my distinct pleasure to welcome Hansib's Jubilee edition of *Guyana at 50: Reflection, Celebration and Inspiration*. This publication provides an exciting tour across Guyana showcasing our people, resources and enterprises, celebrating our achievements and inspiring hopes of a brighter future. As you peruse the pages of this book it is my sincere hope that you begin to sense the pride and attendant euphoria in being able to call Guyana your home.

It is worthy of note that this book is being produced at a time when Guyana celebrates its 50th year as a sovereign state with an abiding commitment to nationhood, social justice, the promotion of cultural plurality and the embracing of ethnicity within the context of a society blessed with a multi ethnic foundation.

Though comprehensive in scope, *Guyana at 50* nevertheless captures the essence of this small South American nation state and as such will delight the potential tourist, the prudent investor, the curious reader or indeed the inquiring researcher in search of relevant up to date information on a still emerging nation state.

The discerning tourist will be happy to experience our abundant waterways, verdant forests, numerous indigenous communities, semi pristine flora and fauna, peaceful heritage sites, alluring city scapes, excellent shopping and exciting entertainment opportunities.

I believe that the glossy pictures and picturesque descriptions are eloquent testimonies of the best of Guyana captured in this book, and I therefore congratulate Hansib Publications on this effort, which is an excellent gesture on the occasion of Guyana's 50th Independence Anniversary Celebrations.

I take this opportunity to invite everyone to join with us as we showcase our country, our people and our collective achievements, for all the world to see and admire.

**Nicolette Henry**
**Minister within the Ministry of Education**
**Responsible for Culture, Youth and Sport**

**Brigadier David Granger**
President of the Co-operative Republic of Guyana

**HON. KHEMRAJ RAMJATTAN, M.P**
Vice President and Minister of Public Security

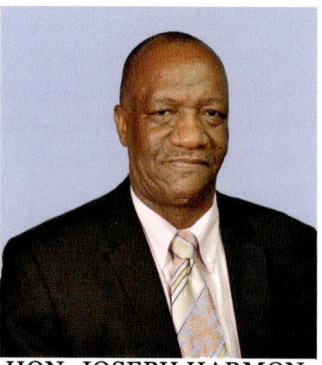

**HON. JOSEPH HARMON**
Minister of State

**HON. Dr. RUPERT ROOPNARAINE**
Minister of Education

**HON. CARL GREENIDGE**
Minister of Foreign Affairs

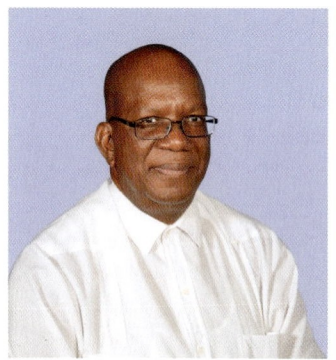

**HON. WINSTON JORDAN**
Minister of Finance

**HON. CATHY HUGHES**
Minister of Tourism

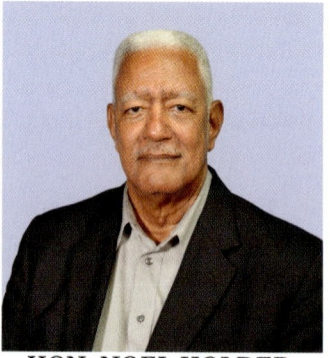

**HON. NOEL HOLDER**
Minister of Agriculture

**HON. Dr. GEORGE NORTON**
Minister of Public Health

**HON. DOMINIC GASKIN**
Minister of Business

**HON. AMNA ALLY**
Minister of Social Cohesion

**HON. RONALD BULKAN**
Minister of Communities

**HON. RAPHEL TROTMAN**
Minister of Governance

**HON. MOSES V. NAGAMOOTOO**
**PRIME MINISTER**
Co-operative Republic of Guyana

**HON. SYDNEY ALLICOCK**
Minister of Indigenous Peoples

**HON. BASIL WILLIAMS**
Minister of Legal Affairs and Attorney General

**HON. DAVID PATTERSON**
Minister of Public Infrastructure

**HON. VOLDA LAWRENCE**
Minister of Social Protection

**HON. WINSTON FELIX**
Minister of Citizenship

**HON. NICOLETTE HENRY**
Minister within the Ministry of Education

**HON. JAIPAUL SHARMA**
Minister within the Ministry of Finance

**HON. SIMONA BROOMES**
Minister within the Ministry of Natural Resources

**HON. KEITH SCOTT**
Minister within the Ministry of Communities

**HON. DAWN HASTINGS-WILLIAMS**
Minister within the Ministry of Communities

**HON. ANNETTE FERGUSON**
Minister within the Ministry of Public Infrastructure

**HON. Dr KAREN CUMMINGS**
Minister within the Ministry of Public Health

# GUYANA

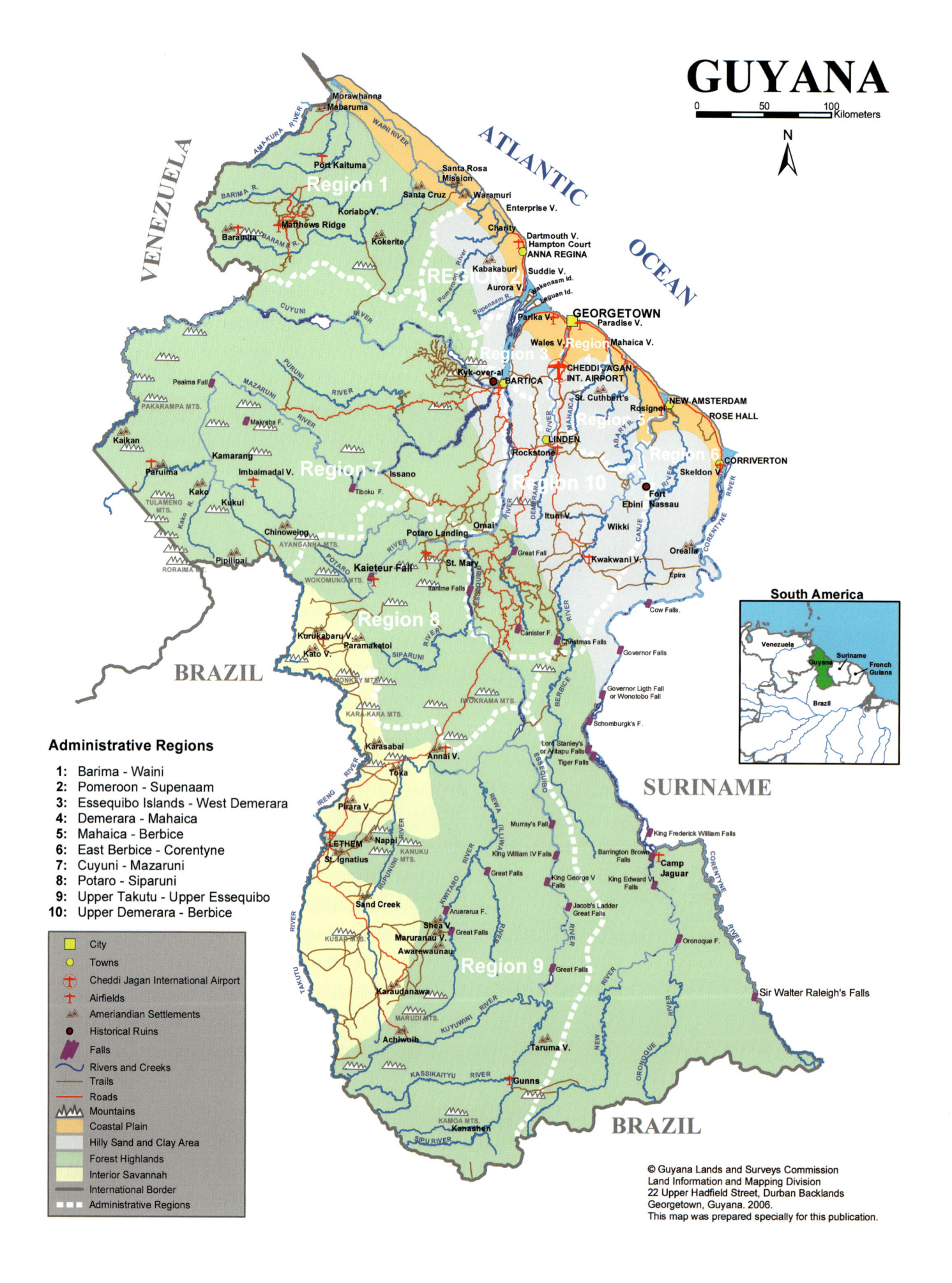

0  50  100 Kilometers

**Administrative Regions**

1: Barima - Waini
2: Pomeroon - Supenaam
3: Essequibo Islands - West Demerara
4: Demerara - Mahaica
5: Mahaica - Berbice
6: East Berbice - Corentyne
7: Cuyuni - Mazaruni
8: Potaro - Siparuni
9: Upper Takutu - Upper Essequibo
10: Upper Demerara - Berbice

**Legend:**
- City
- Towns
- Cheddi Jagan International Airport
- Airfields
- Amerindian Settlements
- Historical Ruins
- Falls
- Rivers and Creeks
- Trails
- Roads
- Mountains
- Coastal Plain
- Hilly Sand and Clay Area
- Forest Highlands
- Interior Savannah
- International Border
- Administrative Regions

South America

© Guyana Lands and Surveys Commission
Land Information and Mapping Division
22 Upper Hadfield Street, Durban Backlands
Georgetown, Guyana. 2006.
This map was prepared specially for this publication.

**Name:** Guyana
**Long form:** Co-operative Republic of Guyana
*Formerly named British Guiana until the nation gained independence from Great Britain on 26 May 1966. The name 'Guiana' is derived from an Amerindian language meaning "land of many waters", and refers to the region's abundance of rivers and streams.*

**Nationality:** Guyanese

**Population:** 735,554 (2014 est.)

**Capital:** Georgetown

**Independence:** Guyana became a Sovereign Nation on 26 May 1966

**Republic:** Guyana became a Republic on 23 February 1970

### Languages
English is the official language and makes Guyana the only South America country whose official language is English. Guyanese Creole (an English-based Creole with linguistic influences and features from West African and Indian languages) is widely spoken. A minority of the population also speak a number of Amerindian languages which include Cariban languages such as Macushi, Akawaio and Wai-Wai; and Arawakan languages such as Arawak (or Lokono) and Wapishana. Hindi, Tamil and Chinese are also spoken. Portuguese is becoming more widely used as a second language particularly in the south of the country bordering Brazil.

### Demographic profile
Guyana is the only English-speaking country in South America and shares cultural and historical bonds with the Anglophone Caribbean. Guyana's two largest ethnic groups are the Indian-Guyanese (descendants of indentured east Indian labourers) and the African-Guyanese (descendants of enslaved Africans). Together, they comprise about three quarters of Guyana's population. The other ethnic groups are Amerindians (9% approx.), Chinese and Europeans

### Religions
Christianity (57%) and Hinduism (28%) are the dominant religions. Other practiced religions and faiths are Islam (7%), Rastafarianism, Buddhism and Baha'i Faith (2%). Around 28% of the population does not profess any religion.

### Location
Guyana is located in northern South America, bordered by Venezuela (western border, 789 km), Brazil (western and southern borders, 1308 km) and Suriname (eastern border, 836 km), with the North Atlantic at its northern coastline (459 km).

### Maritime claims
Territorial sea: 12 nautical miles
Exclusive economic zone: 200 nautical miles

### Area
Total: 214,969 sq km (83,000 sq miles)
Land: 196,849 sq km (76,004 sq miles)
Water: 18,120 sq km (6996 sq miles)

### Climate
Tropical; hot, humid, moderated by north-east trade winds; two rainy seasons – May to mid-August & mid-November to mid-January

**Highest point:** Mount Roraima (2743m / 9000 ft)
*Mount Roraima marks the triple border point of Venezuela (85%), Guyana (10%) and Brazil (5%)*

### Main City & Towns
Georgetown (pop. 124,000)
Linden (pop. 27,280)
New Amsterdam (pop. 17,330)
Anna Regina (pop. 11,780)
Corriverton (pop. 10,600)
Bartica (pop. 8,500)
Rosignol
Skeldon
Vreed en Hoop
Lethem

### Administrative Divisions (ten)
Region 1 - Barima-Waini
Region 2 - Pomeroon-Supenaam
Region 3 - Essequibo Islands-West Demerara
Region 4 - Demerara-Mahaica
Region 5 - Mahaica-Berbice
Region 6 - East Berbice-Corentyne
Region 7 - Cuyuni-Mazaruni
Region 8 - Potaro-Siparuni
Region 9 - Upper Takutu-Upper Essequibo
Region 10 - Upper Demerara-Berbice

**Main rivers**
*Guyana has more than 1500 rivers and over 900 river islands*
Essequibo (630 miles/1010 km)
Berbice (370 miles/595 km)
Demerara (215 miles/346 km)
Potaro (140 miles/225 km)
Pomeroon (one of the deepest rivers in Guyana)
Mazaruni, Kamarang, Puruni, Cuyuni, Siparuni, Burro-Burro, Rupununi, Rewa, Kwitaro, Kuyuwini

**Main waterfalls**
*Guyana has more than 100 waterfalls*
Kaieteur Falls (the world's highest single drop waterfall, 741 ft/226m)
King Edward VIII Falls (840 ft/256m)
Oshi Falls aka King Edward VI Falls (702 ft/214m)
Kumerau Falls (623 ft/190m)
Kamarang Great Falls (525 ft/160m)
Marina Falls (498 ft/152m)
Kurutuik Falls (328 ft/100m)
Amaila Falls (200 ft/60m)
Aruwai Falls (197 ft/60m over 2 km)
Orinduik Falls (82 ft/25m)

**Judicial system**
The common law of Britain is the basis of the legal system in Guyana that has three tiers – Magistrates Courts, the High Court of the Supreme Court of Judicature and the Guyana Court of Appeal. The highest Court of Appeal for civil and criminal matters is the Caribbean Court of Justice.

**Legislature**
Legislative power of Guyana rests in a unicameral National Assembly. Twenty-five members are elected via proportional representation from ten geographic constituencies. Additionally, forty members are chosen, also on the basis of proportional representation, from national lists named by the political parties. The President may dissolve the Assembly and call new elections at any time, but no later than five years from its first sitting.

**Political system**
Parliamentary democracy with executive authority vested in the Head of State

**President** (Head of State & Government)
David Granger (since 16 May 2015)

**Prime Minister**
Moses Nagamootoo (since 20 May 2015)

**Main Political Parties**
A Partnership for National Unity (APNU)
People's National Congress/Reform (PNC/R)
People's Progressive Party/Civic (PPP/C)
Working People's Alliance (WPA)
Alliance for Change (AFC)
Guyana Action Party (GAP)
The United Force (TUF)
Guyana Democratic Party
Justice for All Party
The Unity Party
National Front Alliance
Vision Guyana

**Telephone dialling code:** 592
**Internet country code:** .gy
**Time zone:** GMT -4 hours

**Currency:** Guyana Dollar (GYD, G$, GUY$). US Dollars are also accepted

**Exchange Rate**
USD $1.00 = GYD $207 (2016)
GBP £1.00 = GYD $294 (2016)
CAD $1.00 = GYD $156 (2016)

**GDP per capita:** US $7200 (2015 est.)

**Main export commodities**
Sugar, gold, bauxite, alumina, rice, shrimp, molasses, rum, timber

**Main import commodities**
Manufactures, machinery, petroleum, food

**Membership of international organisations include:**
*Guyana is a full and participating founder member of the Caribbean Community (CARICOM), the headquarters of which are located in the capital, Georgetown*

African Caribbean and Pacific (ACP) countries, Caribbean Court of Justice, Caribbean Development Bank, Community of Latin America and Caribbean States (CELAC), Economic Commission for Latin America and the Caribbean (ECLAC), G-77, Inter-American Development Bank, International Centre for the Settlement of Investment Disputes, International Civil Aviation Organisation, International Development Association, International Finance Corporation, International Fund for Agricultural Development, International Labour Organisation, International Maritime Organisation, International Monetary Fund (IMF), International Olympic Committee (IOC), International Organisation for Standardisation (ISO), International Red Cross and Red Crescent Movement, International Trade Union Confederation, Interpol, Latin American Energy Organisation (OLADE), Latin American and Caribbean Economic System (SELA), MERCOSUR, Non-Aligned Movement, Organization of American States (OAS), Permanent Court of Arbitration, South America/Arab Mechanism (ASPA), South America/Africa Mechanism (ASA), Treaty of Amazonian Co-operation, UNASUR, UNESCO, Union of South American Nations, United Nations (UN), United Nations Conference on Trade and Development (UNCTAD), United Nations Industrial Development Organisation (UNIDO), World Bank, World Health Organisation (WHO), World Intellectual Property Organization, World Trade Organisation (WTO)

# National Anthem of Guyana

*Words by A.L. Luker*  
R.C.G. Potter

Dear land of Guy-a-na, of riv-ers and plains, made rich by the sun-shine and lush by the rains, Set gem-like and fair be-tween moun-tains and sea, Your chil-dren sa-lute you, dear land of the free.

# NATIONAL ANTHEM

## *Dear Land of Guyana, of Rivers and Plains*

*Dear Land of Guyana, of rivers and plains
Made rich by the sunshine and lush by the rains
Set gem-like and fair between mountains and sea
Your children salute you, dear land of the free.*

*Green Land of Guyana, our heroes of yore,
Both bondsmen and free, laid their bones on your shore;
This soil so they hallowed, and from them are we
All sons of one mother, Guyana the free.*

*Great Land of Guyana, diverse though our strains,
We are born of their sacrifice, heirs of their pains;
And ours is the glory their eyes did not see
One land of six peoples, united and free.*

*Dear Land of Guyana, to you will we give
Our homage, our service, each day that we live
God guard you, great Mother, and make us to be
More worthy our heritage – land of the free.*

## The Song of Guyana's Children

*Born in the land of the mighty Roraima,
Land of great rivers and far stretching sea;
So like the mountain, the sea and the river
Great, wide and deep in our lives would we be;*

*Chorus
Onward, upward, may we ever go
Day by day in strength and beauty grow,
Till at length we each of us may show,
What Guyana's sons and daughters can be.*

*Born in the land of Kaieteur's shining splendour
Land of the palm tree, the croton and fern,
We would possess all the virtues and graces,
We all the glory of goodness would learn.*

*Born in the land where men sought El Dorado,
Land of the diamond and bright shining gold,
We would build up by our faith, love and labour,
God's golden city which never grows old.*

*Thus to the land which to us God has given
May our young lives bring a gift rich and rare,
Thus, as we grow, may the worth of Guyana
Shine with a glory beyond all compare.*

CLOCKWISE (from top left): Canje pheasant / RJF; Jaguar / IB; Victoria Amazonica water lily / IB; Coat of Arms; National flag

**National Motto**
"One people. One nation. One destiny."

**National Animal:** Jaguar

**National Bird:** Canje Pheasant (Hoatzin)

**National Flower:** Victoria Amazonica (formerly Victoria Regia) Water Lily

**National Colours:** Red, Yellow, Green, Black and White

**Flag of Guyana**
Green with a red isosceles triangle (based on the hoist side) superimposed on a long, yellow arrowhead; there is a narrow, black border between the red and yellow, and a narrow, white border between the yellow and the green. Green represents the forest, foliage and agriculture; yellow stands for the mineral resources and a bright future; white symbolizes Guyana's rivers; red signifies the zeal and the sacrifices made by the people; black indicates perseverance and endurance.

**Coat of Arms**
*The design of Guyana's Coat of Arms is interpreted as follows:*

The Amerindian headdress symbolises the indigenous people of Guyana; the two diamonds either side of the headdress represent the country's mining industry; the helmet is the monarchical insignia; the two jaguars, holding a pickaxe, a sugar cane and a stalk of rice, symbolise labour and the country's two main agricultural industries - sugar and rice; the shield (decorated with the national flower, Victoria Amazonica lily) is to protect the nation; the three blue wavy lines represent the many waters of Guyana; the canje pheasant at the bottom of the shield is Guyana's national bird.

**National holidays & celebrations**
New Year's Day, 1 January
Republic Day, 23 February (1970)
Mashramani ('Mash'), usually observed on Republic Day
Chinese New Year, January/February
Phagwah / Holi ('Festival of Colours')
Eid-ul-Fitr (End of Ramadan)
Good Friday
Easter Sunday
Easter Monday
Labour Day, 1 May
Arrival Day, 5 May (1838)
Independence Day, 26 May (1966)
Enmore Martyrs' Day, 16 June (1948)
CARICOM Day, 1st Monday in July
Youman Nabi (Birth of the Prophet Mohammed), December
Emancipation Day, 1 August (1834)
Amerindian Heritage Month, September
Deepavali / Diwali ('Festival of Lights')
Eid-ul-Azha ('Feast of Sacrifice')
Christmas Day
Boxing Day

# ADMINISTRATIVE Map Of GUYANA

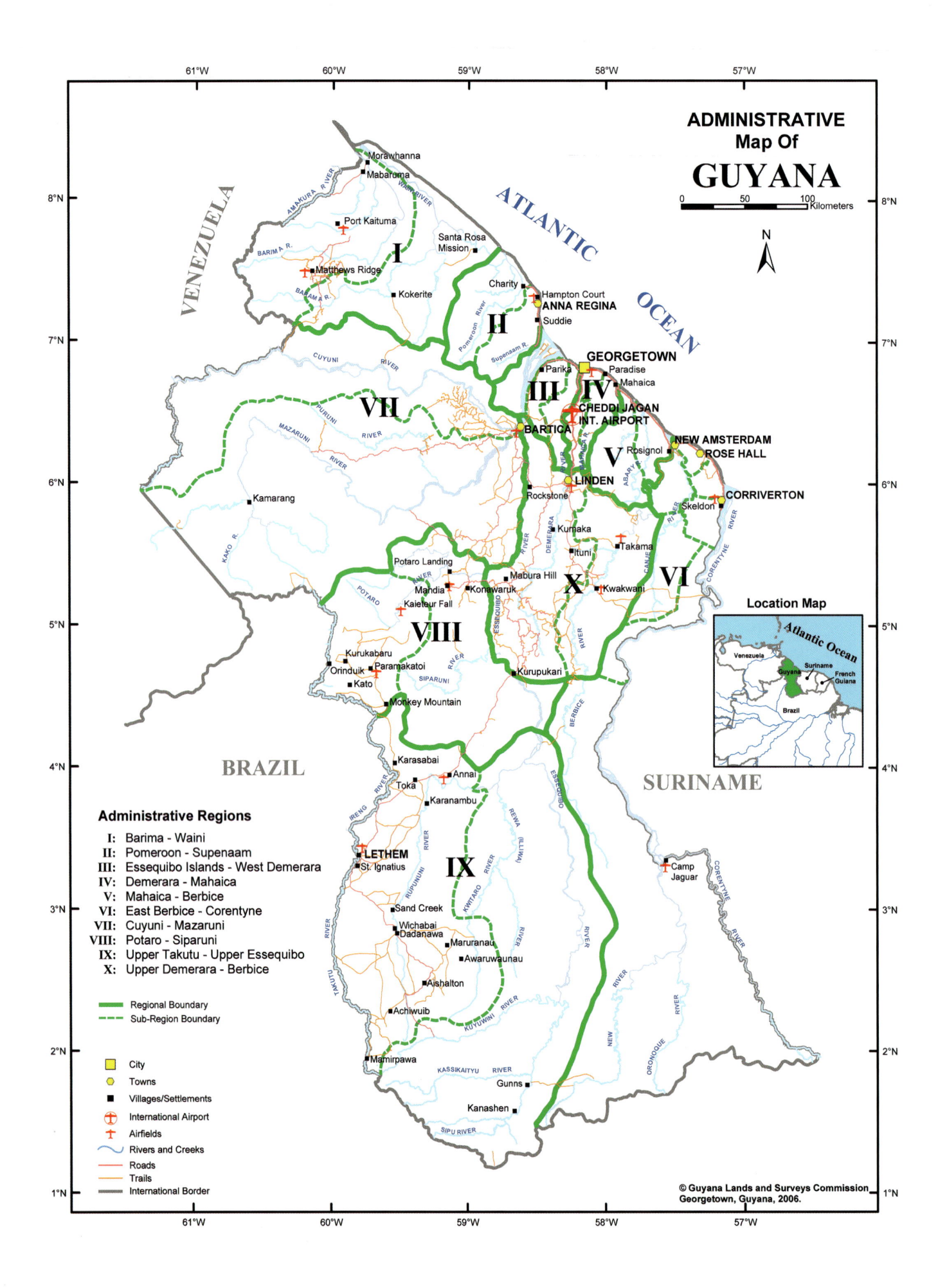

**Administrative Regions**
- I: Barima - Waini
- II: Pomeroon - Supenaam
- III: Essequibo Islands - West Demerara
- IV: Demerara - Mahaica
- V: Mahaica - Berbice
- VI: East Berbice - Corentyne
- VII: Cuyuni - Mazaruni
- VIII: Potaro - Siparuni
- IX: Upper Takutu - Upper Essequibo
- X: Upper Demerara - Berbice

Legend:
- Regional Boundary
- Sub-Region Boundary
- City
- Towns
- Villages/Settlements
- International Airport
- Airfields
- Rivers and Creeks
- Roads
- Trails
- International Border

© Guyana Lands and Surveys Commission
Georgetown, Guyana, 2006.

## SIGNIFICANT EVENTS IN THE HISTORY OF GUYANA

1616 Dutch establish the first colony: Essequibo
1627 Dutch establish the colony of Berbice
1664 First sugar mill established in Essequibo
1752 Dutch establish the colony of Demerara
1763 Berbice Slave Rebellion led by Cuffy
1781 Essequibo, Demerara and Berbice captured by the British
1790 First printing press imported to Demerara
1793 First newspaper launched
1807 Abolition of the Slave Trade Act (effective 1808)
1812 Stabroek renamed Georgetown
1831 The colonies of Demerara, Essequibo and Berbice were united to form the colony of British Guiana
1833 Slavery Abolition Act in the British West Indies (effective August 1834, 'Emancipation')
1835 Arrival of indentured Portuguese
1838 Arrival of indentured Indians
1839 Formation of the Police Force
1842 British Guiana African Association formed
1853 Arrival of indentured Chinese
1916 British Guiana East Indian Association formed
1917 Common Law of England becomes the Common Law of British Guiana
1929 Income Tax introduced
- Kaieteur National Park established
1946 Women's Political and Economic Organisation established
1948 Deaths of five sugar workers in Enmore; now commemorated as Enmore Martyrs Day
1950 People's Progressive Party (PPP) formed
1953 Universal Adult Suffrage introduced
1957 Founding of the People's National Congress (PNC)
1960 Formation of United Force Party
1963 University of British Guiana established
1966 British Guiana (Guyana) gains independence from Great Britain
1970 Guyana becomes a Co-operative Republic
- Privy Council abolished as final court of appeal
1972 First Caribbean Festival of Arts (Carifesta)
1973 Treaty of Chaguaramas is signed establishing CARICOM
1974 Formation of the Working People's Alliance (WPA) with Walter Rodney as leader
1975 Shridath Ramphal appointed second Commonwealth Secretary-General
1977 First Caribbean nation to sign Convention concerning the protection of the World Cultural and Natural Heritage
1987 Guyana Prize for Literature established
1995 Walter Rodney Memorial Park established in Hadfield Street, Georgetown
1996 Joint mandate with the Commonwealth Secretariat to manage the Iwokrama forest
2001 Guyana signs agreement to establish Caribbean Court of Justice
2003 Ethnic Relations Commission established
- Guyana Stock Exchange established
2005 CARICOM's new headquarters inaugurated
- New political party, the Alliance for Change (AFC), is launched
- Prince Charles extends his patronage of the Iwokrama International Centre
2006 Caribbean Single Market Economy (CSME) launched
2007 VAT and Excise Act comes into effect
2010 Government legalises casino gambling
2011 Partnership for National Unity (APNU) formed
2016 Golden Jubilee of Guyana's Independence
- 49th anniversary of the Women's Army Corps
- Centenary of Berbice High School
- Local Government Elections

*Compiled by Petamber Persaud*

---

## PRIME MINISTERS & PRESIDENTS SINCE 1966

### PRIME MINISTERS

**Forbes Burnham** (1923-1985), 26 May 1966 to 6 October 1980
**Ptolemy Reid** (1912-2003), 6 October 1980 to 16 August 1984
**Desmond Hoyte** (1929-2002), 16 August 1984 to 6 August 1985
**Hamilton Green** (1934- ), 6 August 1985 to 9 October 1992
**Samuel Hinds** (1943- ), 9 October 1992 to 17 March 1997
**Janet Jagan** (1920-2009), 17 March 1997 to 19 December 1997
**Samuel Hinds** (1943- ), 19 December 1997 to 9 August 1999
**Bharrat Jagdeo** (1964- ), 9 August 1999 to 11 August 1999
**Samuel Hinds** (1943- ), 11 August 1999 to 20 May 2015
**Moses Nagamootoo** (1947- ), 20 May 2015 to

### PRESIDENTS

**Arthur Chung** (1918-2008), 17 March 1970 to 16 October 1980
**Forbes Burnham** (1923-1985), 6 October 1980 to 6 August 1985 *(died in office)*
**Desmond Hoyte** (1929-2002), 6 August 1985 to 9 October 1992
**Cheddi Jagan** (1918-1997), 9 October 1992 to 6 March 1997 *(died in office)*
**Samuel Hinds** (1943- ), 6 March 1997 to 19 December 1997
**Janet Jagan** (1920-2009), 19 December 1997 to 11 August 1999 *(resigned)*
**Bharrat Jagdeo** (1964- ), 11 August 1999 to 3 December 2011
**Donald Ramotar** (1950- ), 3 December 2011 to 16 May 2015
**David Granger** (1945- ), 16 May 2015 to present

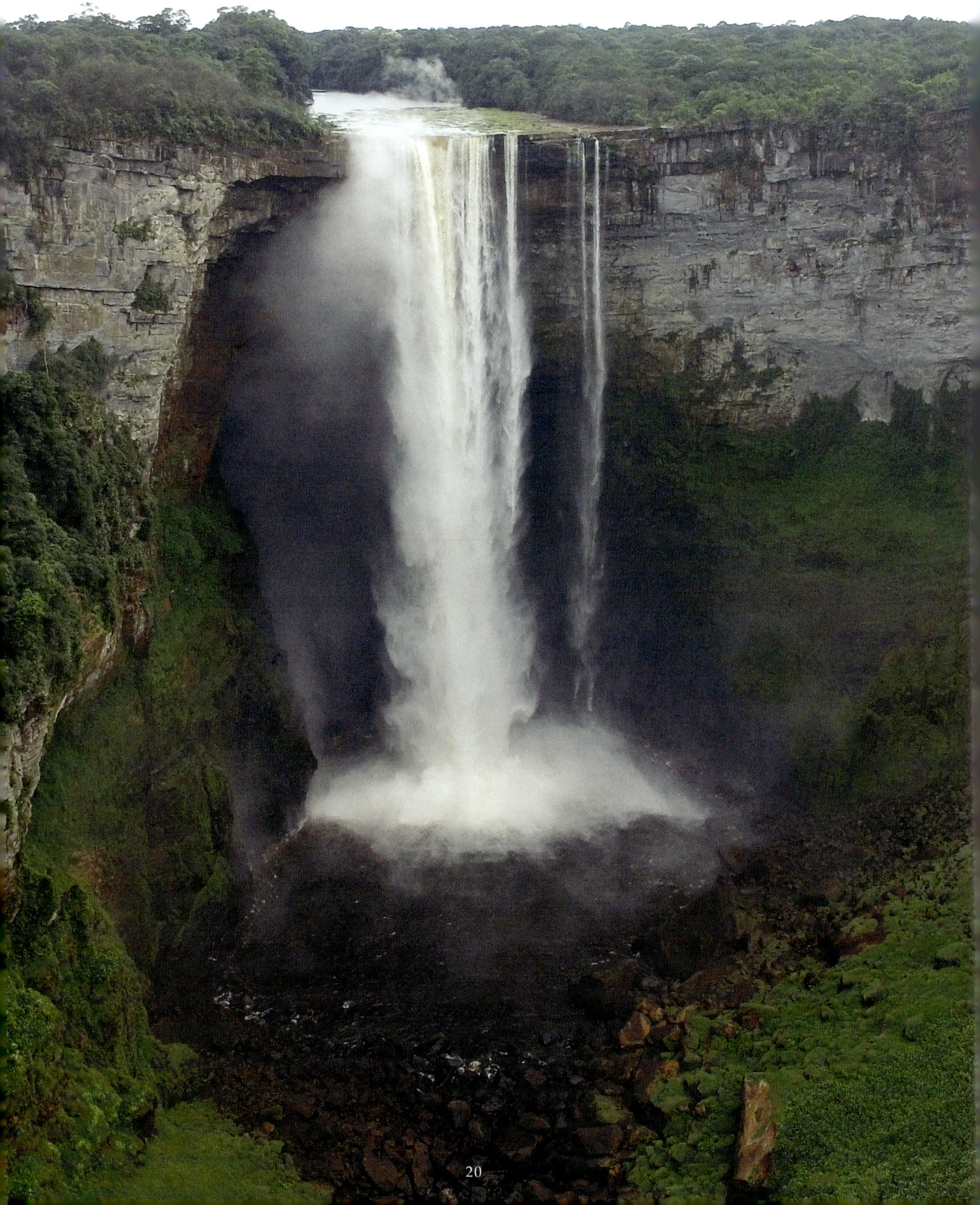

Located on the Potaro River, the magnificent Kaieteur Falls is the world's widest single-drop waterfall. It is also among the most powerful waterfalls in the world. Towering about four times higher than Niagara Falls in North America and about twice the height of Victoria Falls in Africa, this iconic waterfall is part of the Kaieteur National Park in central Guyana / IB

# *A time for reflection, celebration and inspiration*

Guyana, the 'land of many waters' and the only South American country where English is the official language, is blessed with a vast network of waterways, waterfalls and rapids and quite possibly the world's last largely untouched swathe of pristine rainforest covering most of its 83,000 square miles.

Bordered to the east by Suriname, to the south by Brazil and to the west by Venezuela, its shores are washed on the north by the Atlantic Ocean from whence come the northeast trade winds, making this stretch of coastland, on which more than 80 per cent of its population still lives, one of the most beautiful and comfortable on which to dwell. Sitting some seven feet below sea level at the coastline, it is protected along much of its coast, by a sea wall first constructed by the Dutch in the 1880s.

With a population of some 740,000, it has been called the 'mudlands' because of the rich and fertile soil along its coastal belt.

The country was first colonised by the Dutch in the early seventeenth century in their quest to acquire lands akin to those of the other major European powers. However, it was back in 1531, with the arrival of an expedition led by the Spaniard Diego de Ordaz, that Europeans actually set foot on Guyanese soil.

Dutch sovereignty was officially recognised with the signing of the Treaty of Munster in 1648. Over the next 150 odd years the Dutch retained control of the territory but both the French and the English would wrest control at various times with the British finally being ceded the three counties of Essequibo, Demerara and Berbice in 1814. Named British Guiana in 1831, the country would remain under British control until independence in 1966.

First to inhabit these shores were the indigenous peoples the Dutch found living here when they settled in Essequibo. Strictly speaking, there are four main nations among the indigenous inhabitants: Warraus, Arawaks, Wapisianas and Caribs, which include several sub-groups, Arrecunas, Akawaios, Patamonas, Wai-Wais and the Macusis.

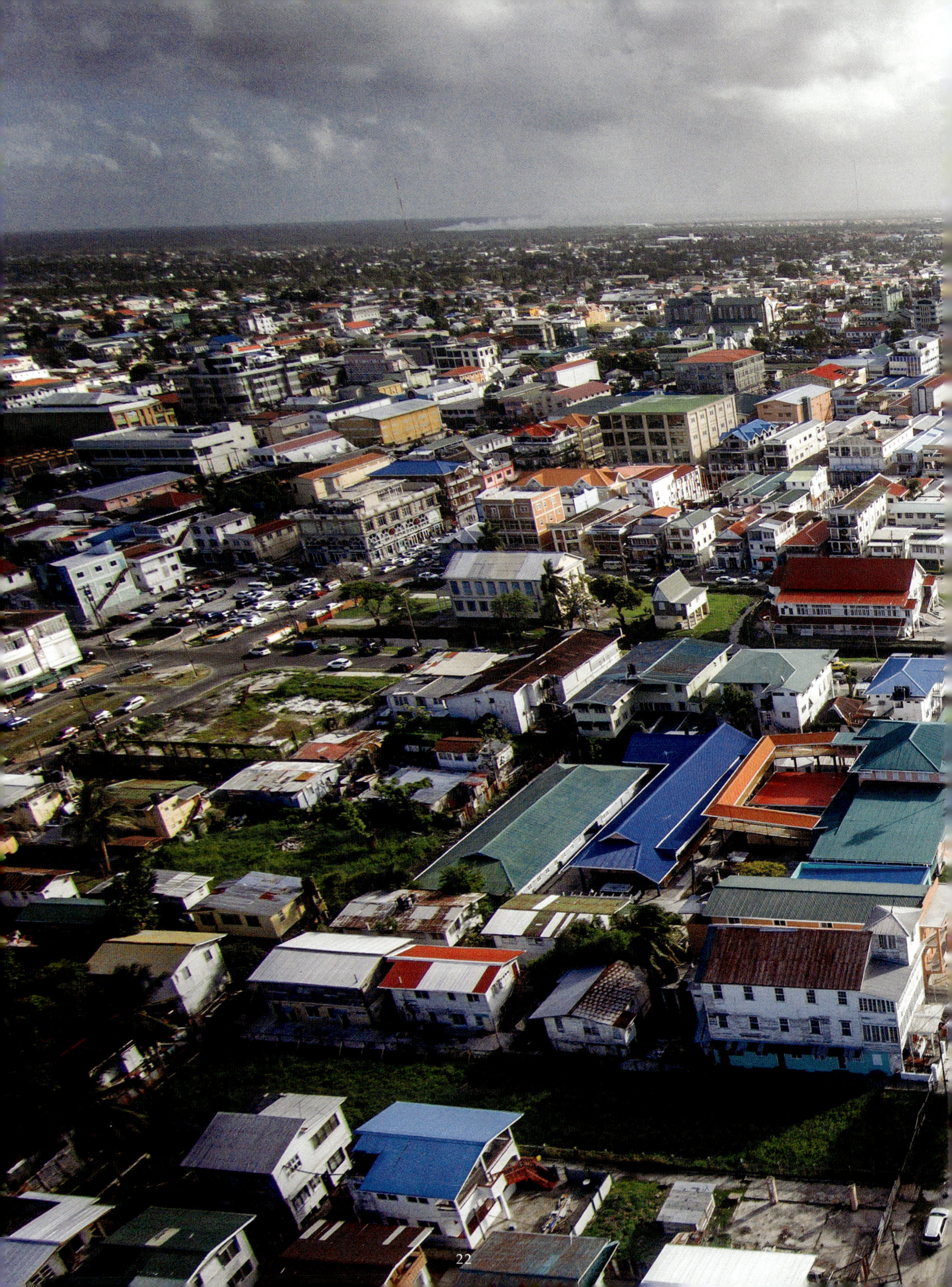

Amid the hustle and bustle of Georgetown stands St George's Cathedral. Guyana's capital is the country's largest urban centre and is located at the mouth of the Demerara River / IB

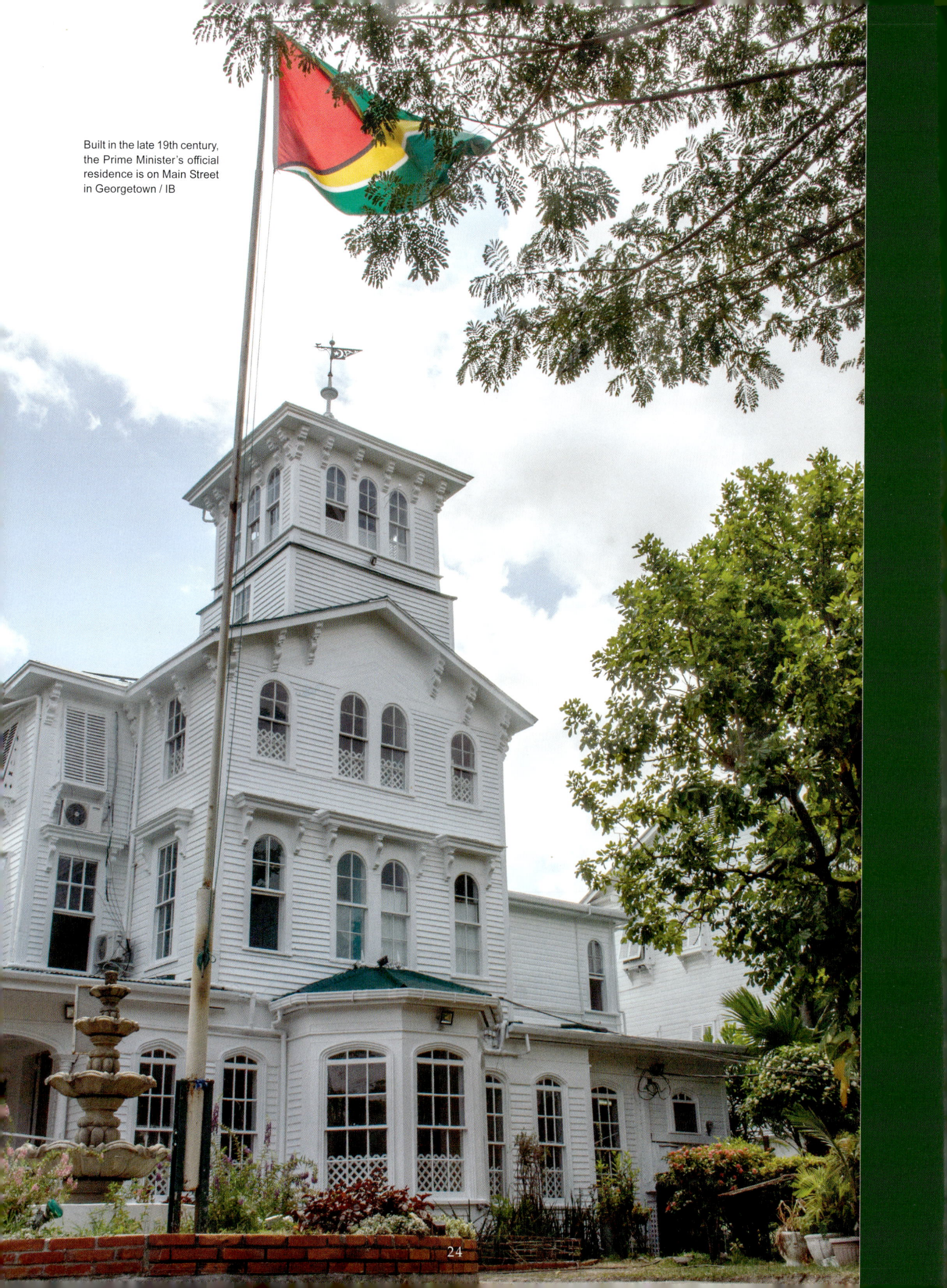

Built in the late 19th century, the Prime Minister's official residence is on Main Street in Georgetown / IB

Education is at the forefront of the Granger administration's thrust for the development of the country – with the leader dubbing himself the "Education President". His deep interest in the sector has been demonstrated by his commitment to ensuring that children, especially those in far flung communities can get to school in his "3 Bs" programme: the provision of buses, boats and bicycles. Already, under his aegis, hundreds of bicycles and several boats and buses are making it possible for students to get to school.

The Ministry of Education is now in the first phase of consultations for educational sector reform, having completed a country-wide audit of schools. The aim is to build an educational system that is responsive to the needs of Guyana's population – from nursery to university.   Pictured: Schoolchildren on Main Street / IB

The next to arrive were the enslaved Africans, brought in the mid-seventeenth century to service the ever-expanding agricultural enterprises set up by the Dutch. The abolition of slavery prompted the need for labour and in 1834 the first group of Portuguese arrived from the island of Madeira.

Small groups of German, English and Irish settlers also came at this time along with other Africans and settlers from neighbouring Caribbean countries. But it was the Indians, arriving on 5th May 1838 from Utter Pradesh and Bihar, who would prove to be the largest contingent of labourers to fuel the system of indentureship proposed by Sir John Gladstone, British Member of Parliament, owner of one of the plantations on West Demerara and father of British Prime Minister William Gladstone.

With the suspension of Indian indentureship that then ended in 1917, the first Chinese arrived in 1851, with the last group coming in 1879.

It was this amalgam, this pot-pourri, this cook-up, which would evolve to become an independent nation. A nation that four years after Independence would declare itself the Co-operative Republic of Guyana and proceed on a course of self-sufficiency with far reaching implications.

Independence was cemented in 1966 with the hoisting of the Golden Arrowhead. This new flag, National Anthem and other national songs, National Pledge and Coat of Arms were all symbols of the emergence of a new sovereign state. The euphoria that accompanied the first tentative steps into this bold new world, a feeling shared by much of the Caribbean at the time, was typified by an outpouring of creativity that would culminate in the first ever Caribbean Festival of the Arts (Carifesta) in 1972, held in Guyana.

The dream of nationhood, predicated on the republican ideal of egalitarianism, was soon

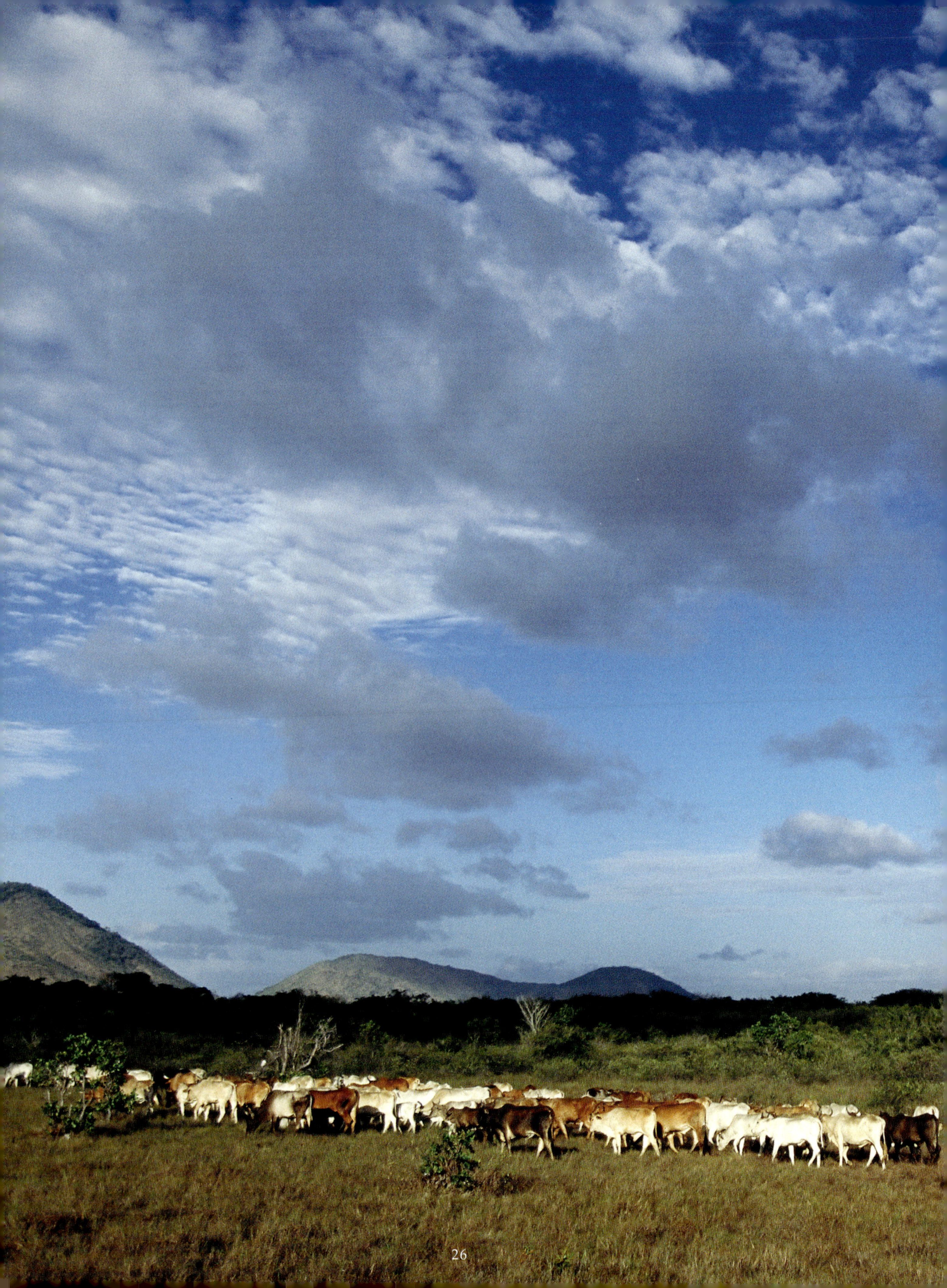

The Rupununi Savannah is located in the south-western region of Upper Takutu-Upper Essequibo (Region 9). The largest of Guyana's ten regions, it is home to tropical and sub-tropical grasslands, savannahs and shrublands. Cattle-ranching is one of the region's leading industries / DW-GTA

The hustle and bustle of Georgetown is no more evident than at Stabroek Market. Vendors both inside and outside the covered market, as well as taxi and minibus operators, compete for business side-by-side / KA

Often compared with Kaieteur Falls, Kumerau Falls is located on the Kurupung River in Guyana's north-western Region 7 (Cuyuni-Mazaruni) / IB

superseded by the reality of the prevailing geopolitical situation. The choice of socialism as the guiding principle for the country's development did not sit well with some in the international community and the pressure to change intensified. Even within this context, Guyana became one of the few countries in the hemisphere to provide free education from nursery to university and free healthcare for all.

Lack of resources and access to new technologies, however, would stymie development and the next years saw a steady decline in services and infrastructure.

The 70s and 80s, considered by many to have been the most challenging for the citizens of Guyana, began an exodus that continues up until the present day. With an already small population, this brain drain has contributed significantly to some of the challenges with which the country is now confronted. Human resource capital is crucial for national development and some of Guyana's best minds now live in the Diaspora. But within this framework there was also forged a resilience and fortitude that typifies the modern Guyanese citizen. They learnt to utilise what was available and many innovations were generated over those years.

Creativity and innovation bloomed as the search continued for solutions to the seemingly endless problems. Staple food was cultivated and a cuisine created using what was available; cotton planted to make locally produced clothes; houses built using materials that were found within the country's borders and other survival strategies developed that surprised many when looking back at what were accomplished.

And many of those who migrated to other countries saw the need to contribute, both to their families that remained and to the development of the country as a whole. Guyana's economy has been buoyed by the exchanges typified by the remittances that have flowed from these sources and the numerous

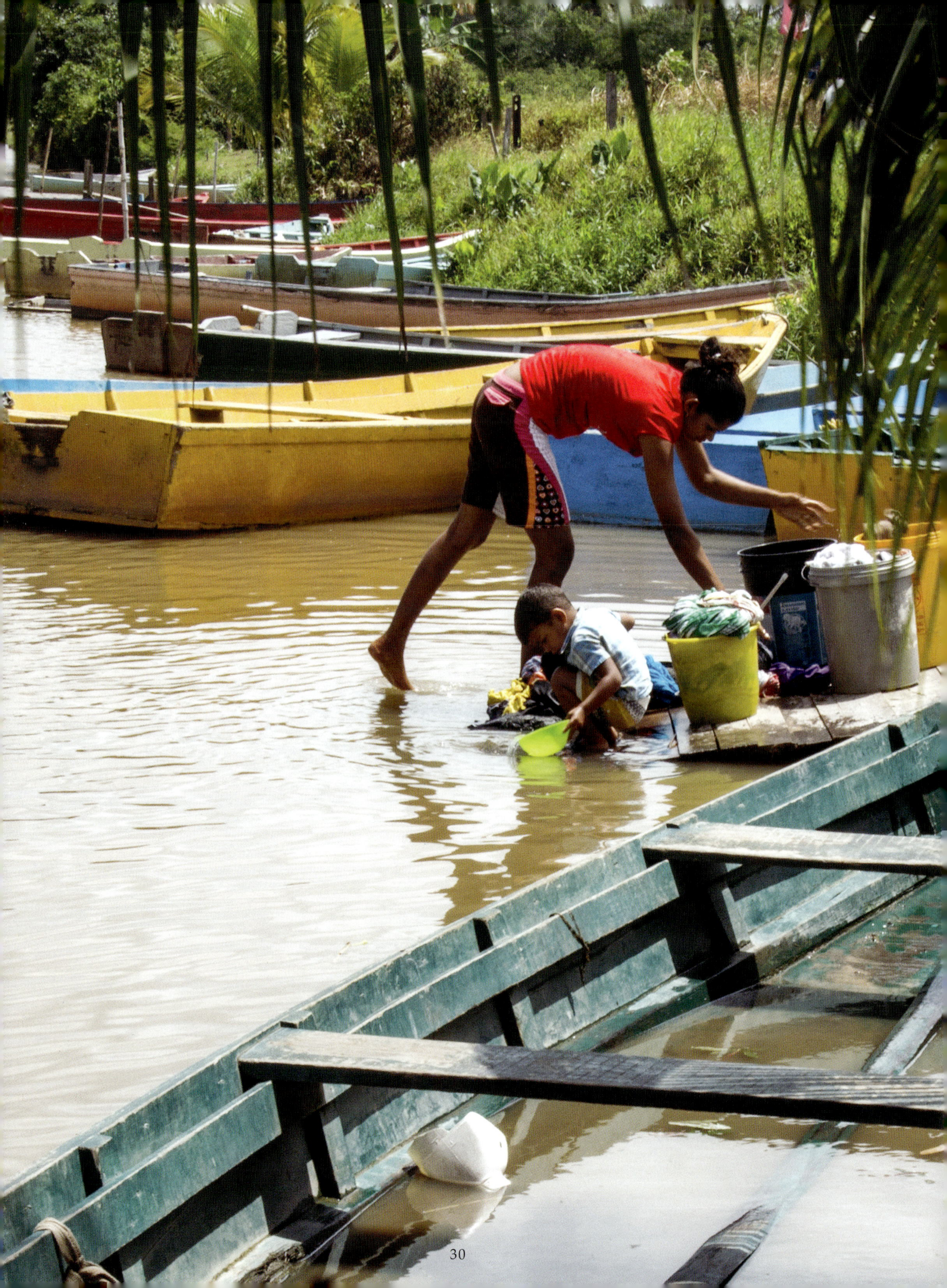

Life in riverain communities differs from that in the cities and towns. The river is for sailing, swimming and sometimes for washing clothes / IB

Members of the various indigenous Guyanese communities travel frequently between neighbouring countries and also create satellite communities both close to and far from established villages / FN-GTA

groups that have initiated programmes: medical visits, educational exchanges and poverty alleviation projects, to name a few, that have eased the strain of living.

The country still remains one of the most beautiful and blessed; the people still renowned for their legendary hospitality. With its numerous waterways and diversity of flora and fauna, Guyana has, without doubt, within its 83,000 square miles some of the most engaging of landscapes. Located in an area that does not experience hurricanes or earthquakes, tornados or tsunamis, flooding is quite possibly the only major natural catastrophe with which Guyana has had to contend. Because the coastal plain, where the vast majority of the population lives, is below sea level, this can be a serious problem on the relatively few occasions when there is protracted rainfall.

This coastal plain is protected from flooding along much of its length by a seawall, canals and kokers which regulate the flow of water according to the tides. Excessive flooding is usually the result of storms that can last for several days and so impede the removal of water from the land facilitated by the drainage network. But because this is not a regular occurrence, ways to cope with the inconvenience have been found when it does occur.

The abundance of fresh produce, sugar and rice, much more than can be consumed, means that with the proper systems and infrastructure the country can indeed become one of the major players in the agricultural sector.

Harnessing its natural resources of gold, bauxite, precious and semi-precious stones and recent finds of oil reserves could be a signal that Guyana is poised for the next phase of its development.

The country stands ready for serious investment.

To Guyanese, the celebration of fifty years of Independence brings with it mixed emotions. There is much to celebrate and much on which to reflect. There is so much more that still needs to be done and so much more that could have been achieved, had there been the will and the resources. The hope, therefore, is that Guyanese will see this as an opportunity to re-evaluate this journey, keep doing the things that have garnered the best results for all and do away with those things that have been inimical to progress as a nation.

It is a time for reflection, celebration and inspiration.

# Guyana Graphic

Midnight—and 152 years of colonial rule is broken

THURSDAY, MAY 26, 1966

# GUYANA'S FLAG IS UP

## GRAPHIC COMMENT

### A NEW EPOCH

THE UNION JACK came down orderly, deliberately, and there was not the slightest hesitancy in its descent.

And it brought down with it into the piled mosaic of history over a century and a half of British colonial administrative rule.

And the five-colour flag of the new nation of Guyana went up, eagerly and with an exultant flutter.

And it took up with it into the costal unknown of the imponderable future the hopes and aspirations of a young nation.

There was a hushed, almost reverent, silence.

A new nation was born.

And it came into being amidst propitious omens of Western and Eastern diplomatic recognition.

From twelve o'clock last night this country was legalistically free. The Guyana Act which was introduced in 1928, and under which the British legislated by Order-in-Council, no longer exists. The heavy responsibility of making decisions which can either make or mar the new nation rests with the government...

has been the responsibility of independence. What took place last night was a symbolic transfer of one to the other.

AT the witching hour of midnight, thousands of Guyanese stood and cheered with restrained joy as their National Flag was raised and the Union Jack was lowered last night.

The ceremony, marking the end of Colonial rule, took place as a crescent moon, sheltered behind dark clouds, formed an impressive background.

### CENTRAL FIGURES

Standing side by side a few feet away from the 40-foot fluttering Guyana flag, Sir Richard Luyt, the first Governor-General of Guyana, and Prime Minister Forbes Burnham became the central figures watching on intently at the symbolic ceremony which ushered in a new era for the people of this former South American British Colony.

Today the nation's five-colour flag flutters proudly in more than 150 villages and towns stretching from Mount Ayanganna in the Pakaraimas to Manchester on the Corentyne.

In a riot of Guyana colours, the people had formed the biggest assembly in the whole history of the country to welcome the birth of their nationhood.

### LONG CHEERS

They gave long cheers to three very important persons, who had, in their own way, made last night's ceremony the unique and significant occasion it was—Prime Minister Burnham, Opposition Leader, Dr. Cheddi Jagan, and former Tory Colonial Secretary, Mr. Duncan Sandys, the man who introduced Proportional Representation here.

Mr Burnham and Dr Jagan...

### ROUSING APPLAUSE

ceremony was cut by half, and even more disappointing, steelbands were told that there would be no tramping until Monday night.

But the crowds were too happy to be angry. They danced their way out of the Queen Elizabeth Park, and moved like a flood tide through the City streets.

Guyana has now become the 23rd member of the Commonwealth of nations.

Admission to the Commonwealth was announced yesterday by Mr. Arnold Smith, Commonwealth Secretary-General, on the authority of the Commonwealth

Colonial Secretary, Mr. Fred Lee, successor to Mr. Anthony Greenwood, who presided over the conference which wrote the final chapter to the country's march to freedom, last night despatched his congratulations to the new nation.

### NEW PARTNERS

"We welcome you" he said, "as new partners in the Commonwealth. We are confident that we are entering a new and even stronger association between our two countries. I send to the people of Guyana my very best wishes in their task of building a stable and a prosperous future."

DOWN AND UP: Lights were dimmed as thousands of eyes watched the ceremony in which the Union Jack came down and the Flag of Guyana went up to herald the birth of the new nation. The two flags are seen touching each other on their respective journeys. (Picture by DONALD PERIANA).

## G-G HAS 'VAST FAITH' IN GUYANA'S FUTURE

GUYANA'S first Governor-General, Sir Richard Luyt, said yesterday that he had "considerable confidence in the future of the new nation." He was at the time meeting foreign and... in his capacity... eight hours be... flag was unveiled... Elizabeth Park... a number... internal and ex... and also de... that he would... regard as his greatest achievement, or greatest failure during his past two years as Governor.

The foreign newsmen asked many questions relating to the state of emergency and continued detention of nine per...

security of the country.

As of now, he added, he was merely affixing his signature to documents relating to detention or release of persons. He was acting on the advice of his Ministers.

Answering a question on what he regarded as the outstanding achievements of British Colonial rule here, Sir Richard said, in one word, "Health." He then explained the successful campaign to rid the country of the scourge of malaria, the establishment of the Leprosarium at Mahaica and the hospital for tuberculosis cases at Best on the West Coast, Demerara.

He said he would not say that because of colonialism, these problems in the field of health existed, but there had been a statement explaining the difference between his role as Governor and that as Governor-General.

## PM TO MEET THE DELEGATES

THE importance of social and economic integration in the Caribbean, closer trade and cultural and other links with Africa and Asia will be discussed informally today and Saturday by Prime Minister Forbes Burnham, and visiting delegates from the Caribbean, Africa and Asia...

---

"Mr Burnham and Dr Jagan surprised and delighted the crowds with a warm embrace some 1 ½ hours before the union Jack was hauled down and the Guyana flag hoisted." Extract from the front page of the *Guyana Graphic* newspaper of Thursday, 26 May 1966

# The long road to Independence

Guyana was a colony of The Netherlands and Great Britain for over 350 years. It was first colonized by the Dutch and was ceded to the British by the Treaty of London in 1814.

Many colonies all over the world began to demand their independence from Belgian, Dutch, French, Spanish and Portuguese empires from the end of the Second World War. The antecedents of the Independence movement in the British West Indies, however, predated the end of the Second World War and had their roots deeply embedded in the West Indian workers experience at the end of the First World War in the 1920s and 1930s.

The awakening of anti-colonial thinking and the growth of national consciousness in Guyana followed the paths of trade unionism, political empowerment and constitutional change, particularly the introduction of the universal adult franchise.

TRADE UNIONISM

Trade unionism, driven by the militancy of thousands of workers across the British West Indies (BWI), had the most direct influence on the Independence movement. Guyana's first trade union was founded for, and by, urban waterfront workers whose employment was irregular and who were wholly dependent on their wages for their subsistence.

Hubert Critchlow was the celebrated labour leader and founder of the British Guiana Labour Union (BGLU) in 1919. The Union was registered in 1922. Workers' standards of living, at that time, were being eroded by the inflation and depression which inevitably afflicted the colonies in the wake of major European wars, in this case, the First World War. The BGLU became the true archetype of the later mass-based political parties.

Hubert Critchlow was a founding member of the British Guiana and West Indies Labour Conference, held in January of 1926, which later gave birth to the Caribbean Labour Congress. He was one of the pioneers of the movement towards self-government and independence in British Guiana. It was the trade unions which first and most frequently confronted foreign-owned plantation, mining, shipping and other commercial interests, setting the stage for the anti- colonial struggle.

The unionisation and mobilisation of workers had a great impact on political change during what is known, historically, as the 'Labour Rebellion' which occurred all across the BWI between 1934 and 1939. A series of strikes, riots and other forms of disorder, starting in British Honduras in 1934, affected Antigua, The Bahamas, Barbados, Jamaica, St Kitts, St Lucia, St Vincent and Trinidad and Tobago and culminated in British Guiana in 1939. More than thirty people were killed and over one hundred injured during this rebellion.

The 'Labour Rebellion' in the British West Indies and British Guiana resulted in the appointment of the West Indian Royal Commission – led by Lord Moyne and known as the 'Moyne Commission'. The Commission visited Guyana from 27th January to 20th February 1939, just about the time that labour disturbances occurred on Plantation Leonora on the West Coast of Demerara.

The Royal Commission was charged with investigating and making recommendations on the social and economic conditions in the territories. The Commission also examined, among other things, the political system operating in all the territories and recommended the expansion of the franchise enabling people other than the well-to-do and the educated to stand for election. It completed its Report in 1940 but the British Government did not publish it until July 1945, after the Second World War ended.

British colonial policy, particularly after the publication of the Report of the 'Moyne Commission' also started to veer towards independence. The Secretary of State for the Colonies announced in 1945, "The declared aim

Celebrated labour leader and founder of the British Guiana Labour Union, Hubert Critchlow

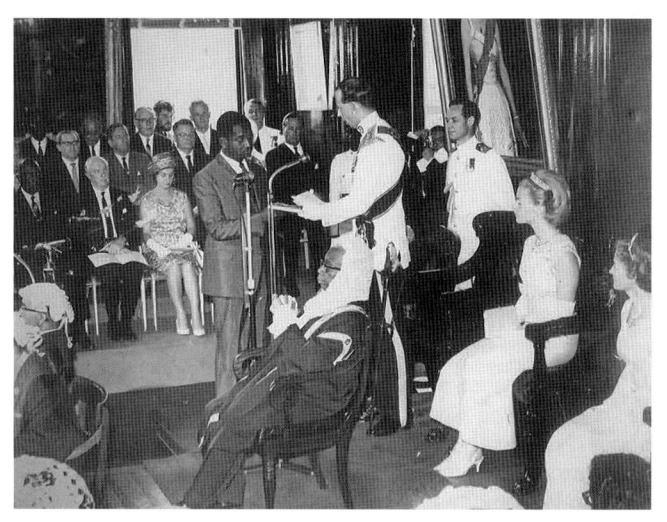

Prime Minister Forbes Burnham accepts the instuments of independence from the Duke of Kent / *Stabroek News*

of British policy is to quicken the progress of all colonial peoples towards the ultimate goal of self-government… I take this opportunity of reaffirming this basic aim in relation to the Caribbean area."

POLITICAL EMPOWERMENT

Political empowerment was another pathway towards Independence. The earliest steps were taken, tentatively, from the time of the general elections of 1921 with the formation of the British Guiana People's Political Association (BGPPA). The Association was a mere proto-party, concerned principally with the short-term objectives of supporting candidates for elections to the Combined Court, as the legislature was called at that time.

The Association's example influenced the formation of the more successful Popular Party in 1926. The populism and relative radicalism of candidates helped to precipitate the suspension of the quasi-representative Constitution and the imposition of a reactionary regime in 1928. The British Guiana Labour Party (BGLP) was another multi-ethnic proto-party. The BGLP, in the general elections held in 1947, won six of the fourteen seats in the Legislative Council.

The formation of the original PPP in 1950 marked another step on the road towards national Independence. The original People's Progressive Party (PPP) was a party of the new type which benefited from the mass consciousness stimulated by the trade union movement and the progressive policies proposed by the proto-parties which had emerged during the previous thirty years. It was Guyana's first modern, mass-based party. Its success at the general elections of 1953 was attributed, largely, to the leadership of Forbes Burnham and Cheddi Jagan and to its superior organisation.

Theophilus Lee, the first President of the British Guiana Trade Union Congress (BGTUC), introduced a motion in the Legislative Council on 25th August 1948 for a commission to be appointed to inquire into the desirability of making the Council a wholly-elected body based on universal adult suffrage and of self-government being granted to the colony. The Council passed a resolution requesting the Governor to appoint a commission to consider the question of reform. He was able to announce in the Legislative Council, on 16th December, that the Secretary of State had agreed to appoint an independent constitutional commission. This Commission – known popularly as the Waddington Commission – was appointed, "to review the franchise, the composition of the Legislative Council and the Executive Council… in light of the economic and political development of the colony and to make recommendations."

The Commission took the view that "neither a property qualification nor a simple literacy test…" could be sufficient criteria to be an elector. It recommended the abolition of both criteria and the introduction of universal adult suffrage. This recommendation was implemented in March 1952.

CONSTITUTIONAL REFORMS

The next constitutional step on the road to Independence was the introduction of the first 'democratic' constitution – familiarly called the 'Waddington Constitution' in 1952. Elections were held under this constitution in April 1953. The original PPP won the majority of seats in the Legislative Council and provided all of the elected Ministers. The British government, however, on Friday 9th October 1953, dismissed the government Ministers who had been in office for only 133 days, suspended the Constitution and sent troops into Georgetown. This was a serious setback on the road to Independence.

The re-introduction of a democratic constitution in 1956 was followed by free elections in 1957. The original PPP, by this time, had split into two factions – one led by Forbes Burnham (the Burnhamites) and the other led by Cheddi Jagan (the Jaganites). Forbes Burnham changed the name of his group to the People's National Congress (PNC) in 1957. Peter D'Aguiar formed the United Force (UF) in 1960.

The introduction of a constitution providing for limited 'self- government' was next. Three parties contested the elections in 1961. The PPP

Cheddi Jagan was leader of the original People's Progressive Party

Prime Minister, Linden Forbes Sampson Burnham unveils Independence Arch on 22 May 1966 marking the birth of Guyana as an independent nation. The arch was a gift to the people of Guyana from the Demerara Bauxite Company.

won the largest amount of seats in the Legislative Assembly and formed the administration. The economy, however, started to show signs of strain by the early 1960s. The cost of living was rising steadily but wages stagnated; workers' morale was low and the migration of skilled people started. The PPP Administration introduced a budget that included several harsh measures which fell unfairly on urban workers. Protests and strikes started, leading to the major riot of 16th February 1962.

The following year, 1963, the PPP Administration attempted to introduce the Labour Relations Bill which triggered such opposition among the trade unions that a general strike was called from 20th April and lasted eighty days, perhaps the longest strike in the Anglophone Caribbean. The strike ended only when the Administration agreed to withdraw the Bill.

The major political leaders – Cheddi Jagan, Forbes Burnham and Peter D'Aguiar – and their advisers once again travelled to London on 22nd October 1963 to discuss constitutional advance and Independence. The PNC and UF called for the introduction of the proportional representation (PR) electoral system and fresh elections before Independence. The PPP called for the retention of the 'first-past-the post' electoral system and the reduction of the voting age to eighteen years. There was deadlock.

The British Secretary of State for the Colonies, Edwin Duncan Sandys, broke the deadlock by introducing the 'PR' system, retaining the voting age of twenty-one years and ordering fresh elections to be called before Independence. This angered the PPP leadership which launched what Cheddi Jagan called a "Hurricane of Protest".

Violence started after the Guiana Agricultural Workers' Union (GAWU) called a strike ostensibly for recognition by the Sugar Producers' Association (SPA) in the sugar industry. The first half of 1964 was taken up with a near civil war, confined largely to the sugar-growing areas. In the mayhem which followed, 176 people were killed; over one thousand were injured; 15,000 people were made homeless or became internal refugees and 1,500 homes or other properties were burnt or destroyed. The GAWU strike was called off in July and normalcy returned after elections were held in December 1964.

The British Guiana (Constitution) Order, 1964, established a House of Assembly as a unicameral legislature, consisting of 53 members elected in accordance with a system of proportional representation. General elections were held under this system that resulted in the displacement of the PPP from office by a coalition of the PNC and UF parties in 1964. The PPP boycotted the Independence constitutional conference in London in 1965.

The British Parliament's Guyana Independence Act 1966, removed UK Government responsibility, renamed the colony 'Guyana' and empowered the Guyana Legislature to make laws for governing the new State. The National Assembly and Supreme Court were established and a Governor General and Prime Minister were appointed.

The British government relinquished "... responsibility for the government of the territory which immediately before that day constitutes the Colony of British Guiana and which on or after that day is to be called Guyana."

Guyana became an independent State on 26th May 1966, after having been the colony of the Dutch and British for over 350 years. Guyana came to the end of a long, hard road to Independence and entered the international community as a free state.

---

Abridged and amended by David A. Granger from his books, *Guyana's Independence 1966* and *The Independence Movement 1946-1966*

Jubilant crowds at Durban Park during the Republic Day flag-raising ceremony on 23 February 2016 / MED

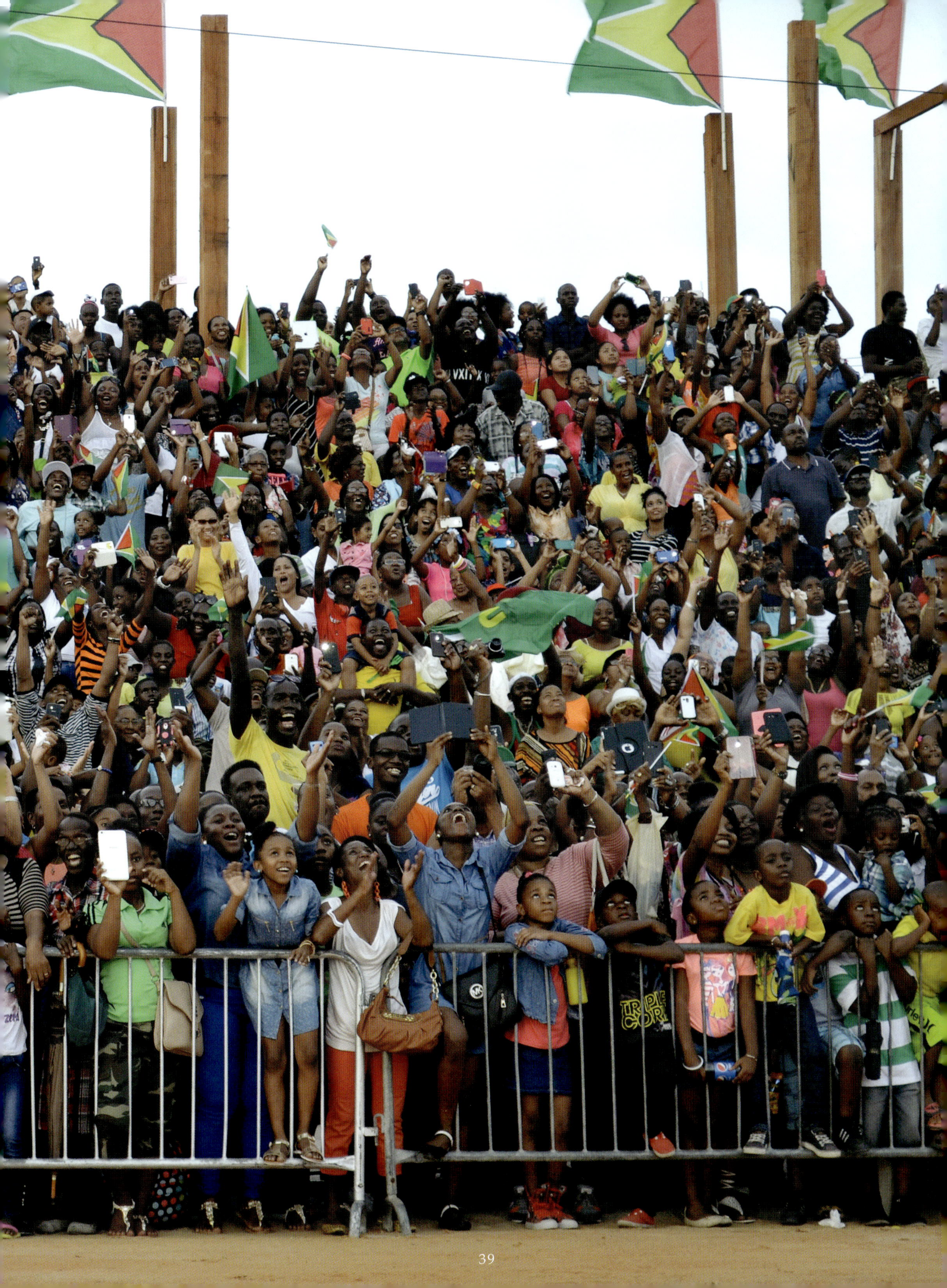

# A brief history of Guyana

The provision of exact dates in history is often the subject of a great deal of controversy, and in the case of Guyana's earliest history, this is no exception. In any event it is perhaps true to say that somewhere around the 1570s non-Spanish Europeans began to take an increasing interest in exploring the Guianas as part of their challenge to Spain's New World monopoly. Moreover, in 1581, the Netherlands renounced its allegiance to Spain and this act of defiance impelled her to investigate and explore trading opportunities in the region.

The limited available evidence seemingly points to the notion that the earliest settlement was established on the Pomeroon by the end of the sixteenth century when Dutch vessels were sent out of the province of Zeeland. Hartsinck speaks of a settlement, Nova Zeelandia, established shortly after 1596 by Dutchman, Joost van der Hooge. This post, although attacked by the Spanish, paved the way for the emergence of similar ones in other parts of the country.

By the truce of Antwerp in 1609, a twelve-year armistice came into being between Spain and the Netherlands and this helped to protect Dutch settlements from further aggression. In 1613, Kyk-over-al was established by Van der Hooge on a small island at the confluence of the Essequibo, Mazaruni and Cuyuni rivers. This settlement became the first durable one under Adrianensen Van Groenwegel and it was strategically located in terms of defence. Kyk-over-al showed early signs of progress and it was boosted with the formation of the Dutch West India Company in 1621. This company assumed immediate control of the settlement and the Dutch also turned their attention towards Berbice. In 1627, Abraham Van Pere was granted permission to colonise the area.

In the initial period, these settlements acted as trading posts for the thriving barter trade which emerged with the native inhabitants. Axes, knives, cloth, beads, trinkets and scissors were exchanged for cotton, hammocks, annatto, tobacco and other products. The Dutch, in order to maximise benefits out of the trading activity, entered into a deliberate policy of appeasement with these indigenous people.

As the settlements took root the Dutch extended their activity to tobacco, coffee and cotton cultivation to ensure these commodities were available in commercial quantities. To this end, the Dutch West India Company began to supply the colonists with enslaved Africans. More land came under cultivation and new settlements emerged, especially on the lower Essequibo. Berbice grew steadily under the patronage of the Van Peres.

Certain events around the mid-seventeenth century had pronounced effects on the future of Essequibo and the country in general. Firstly, by the Treaty of Munster in 1648, Spain officially recognised the independence of the Netherlands. Then, in the early 1650s, the Dutch West India Company declared its intention to allow private individuals, as distinct from the company, to settle in Essequibo. Of even greater significance was the eventual re-conquest of Brazil by the Portuguese. These developments led to an influx of Dutch settlers to Essequibo with much needed capital and expertise. Sugar cane cultivation started on an export basis and Kyk-over-al was transformed from a trading post to a central market. The colonies continued to experience "adverse fortunes of war which led them to a precarious level of existence". The French, under Du Casse, attacked Berbice and Pomeroon in 1689; Essequibo suffered at the hands of Antoine Ferry in 1708-1709 and in 1712 Berbice was bombarded by Jacques Cassard. During these attacks, heavy ransoms were demanded from the Dutch.

Following the attacks on Berbice, administration of the colony was placed in the hands of some Amsterdam merchants who subsequently formed a joint-stock company, the Berbice Association. In 1718, the Council of Policy and Justice became the most important political institution in Essequibo. Both colonies recovered rapidly from the French attacks and by the 1730s more lands along the sea coast were put under sugar, coffee and cotton cultivation. In the case of Essequibo, its larger islands experienced a proliferation of estates.

Dutch colonisation was greatly enhanced through the strenuous efforts of Laurens Storm Van Gravensande who became Commander of Essequibo in 1743. He quickly embarked on a "deliberate and thoughtful policy of development and exploration of Demerara". He obtained permission for settlers from abroad to assist in the venture and the result was an influx of Englishmen from Barbados and Antigua with the necessary capital and expertise. Groups of German, Spanish, French, Swedish and Danish settlers took up the challenge. It was this marked migration to Demerara that gave rise to the unchallenged dominance of the sugar industry for several decades as it "laid the foundation of the wealthy plantocracy".

Such was the phenomenal rise of the new colony, Demerara, that by 1769 it had 206 plantations and 5,967 slaves as compared to 92 plantations and 3,986 slaves in Essequibo. Regarding its growing prosperity, Gravesande revealed, "When one returns to Demerara after a year's absence one is astonished at the progress that has been made." In 1774, its capital, Borselen, was removed to the present capital site and renamed Stabroek.

Meanwhile, in 1763, Berbice was rocked by a major slave uprising. Chronic shortages of supplies, cruel treatment and a fierce desire for freedom were among the principal causes of the revolt. For several weeks the rebels, under Cuffy, were evidently gaining the upper hand in the confrontation as plantation after plantation fell into their hands. In the end, a lack of sustained attacks, disunity and the timely arrival of reinforcements all contributed to a reversal of the situation with the Dutch regaining control.

In 1781, the British captured Essequibo, Demerara and Berbice. This was the beginning of a period of uncertainty and fluctuating fortunes as the colonies were tossed back and forth. In 1783, the French seized them but they were eventually restored to the Dutch. They were again captured by the British in 1796 and occupation lasted until 1802 with restoration to the Dutch. The following year, the British completed their final conquest of the colonies. Formal cession was effected by the 1814 Treaty of Paris. In 1831, the colonies were united into the "colony of British Guiana" and Stabroek was renamed Georgetown.

The British inherited the Dutch system of government and this remained in force until 1891. Such a situation persisted through Article 1 of the 1803 capitulation treaty which stated that the colonies were to retain the existing laws, customs and political institutions.

The abolition of the slave trade in 1807 and slave emancipation in 1834 brought fear, uncertainty and gloom to the plantocracy. This state of affairs worsened with the termination of the apprenticeship system in 1838 as there was a marked exodus of former slaves from the plantations to newly acquired villages and a consequential loss of labour. The village movement quickly gained momentum and by around 1850 over 42,000 former slaves were in the newly created villages which emerged throughout the coastal belt. Added to this, planters began to feel the effects of the 1846 Sugar Duties Act which ended their monopoly on the British market. The grave labour shortage led to the importation of indentured labourers. In the initial years of change and crisis, small numbers of European immigrants including those of German, Irish, English, Scottish, Welsh and Maltese nationalities were brought in, but these failed to make any significant impact on the plantations. As early as 1835, forty Portuguese immigrants were introduced from Madeira and this was followed by a group of 429 a year later.

State-aided Portuguese immigration commenced in 1841 and lasted until 1882 by which time over 31,000 had arrived. Many of these immigrants eventually branched off into commercial activities. Immigration of Africans was encouraged by the British Government and between 1841 and 1863, 14,060 mostly "liberated Africans" from Sierra Leone and St Helena came to the colony. Creole immigrants were also tried and a steady stream of Barbadians, estimated at 40,656, arrived between 1835 and 1893. This type of labour had "qualitative advantages" as it provided a relatively cheap source of experienced labourers. Chinese immigration was another experiment. Between 1853 and 1913, 15,720 Chinese came to the colony.

East Indian immigrants greatly outnumbered all other groups. Under the 'Gladstone experiment', the first group from India arrived in May 1838, but ill-treatment, sickness and high mortality rate led to a temporary suspension of the scheme. Large-scale immigration began around the mid-nineteenth century and lasted until 1917. By that time, over 239,000 immigrants had arrived. In the main, it was this source of East Indian indentured labour that saved the sugar industry from complete collapse in the nineteenth century.

The 1856, Portuguese riots, during which business places were attacked, cast a cloud over future race relations, while the 1870 sighting of Kaieteur Falls by Charles Barrington Brown subsequently brought fame to the colony. Gold was discovered in significant quantities in the 1870s and the gold industry made tremendous strides under the administrations of Henry Irving and Lord Gormanston during the last decades of the century. Increasing numbers of concessions to interior locations were granted to the several gold mining companies which emerged.

This period also witnessed improved techniques in both sugar cane cultivation and in sugar manufacture. The local industry faced the challenge by changing over from muscovado processing to that of vacuum pan manufacture. This latter process involved steam heating and boiling at a lower temperature than before and it led to a greater quantity of crystallised sugar being produced. Such was the transformation that the industry was described as "technologically most advanced" in the region.

In the area of education, 1876 marked the year when the Compulsory Education Bill was introduced. Under it the labouring class was compelled to send their children to school. Schools fell into two categories: (a) 'aided schools' which were under the management of religious bodies, and (b) 'colonial schools' which were under direct government supervision.

By the 1890s, there was a gradual movement from the estates as East Indian immigrants began to buy, rent or even squat on lands along the coastal plain. This process accelerated from the turn of the century and within a few decades many immigrant settlements emerged in the rural districts and these became inextricably bound up with the emergent rice industry.

In 1891, after years of struggle, the constitution underwent major reform. Some of the material changes included the enlargement of the Court of Policy, the abolition of the College of Electors, direct election of the unofficial section of the Court of Policy, the widening of the franchise and the right of the Governor to dissolve the Court of Policy at any time. As gold exploitation intensified in the 1890s, uneasiness appeared in the Venezuelan camp. Venezuela's relationship with Great Britain became strained. This situation led to an international tribunal to define the boundary between British Guiana and Venezuela and hence the Arbitral Award of 1899. Immediately before the colony attained independence in 1966, Venezuela revived her claim to the Essequibo territory and deemed the 1899 award "null and void". This controversy resulted in the 1966 Mixed Commission and the Protocol of Port of Spain, which was terminated in 1982.

A series of strikes gripped the colony in the early twentieth century as workers found it hard to survive. Working class organisation was boosted with the formation of the British Guiana Labour Union in 1919 by the "Father of Trade Unionism in the British Caribbean," Hubert Nathaniel Critchlow. This was followed by an upsurge of trade unions. Agitation for further political reform led to Crown Colony status in 1928 as the Court of Policy and Combined Court were replaced by a Legislative and Executive Councils.

In 1946, Dr Cheddi Jagan, a dentist, founded the Political Affairs Committee, an organisation primarily aimed at fostering political awareness of the masses. Shortly afterwards, he won a seat in the Legislative Council. In 1950, Jagan teamed up with Forbes Burnham, a barrister, and other leaders to form the People's Progressive Party. Elections were held under a new constitution in 1953 and the party swept to power. That triumph was, however, only short-lived. The fear of Communist threat caused Great Britain to suspend the constitution, dispatch troops and declare a state of emergency. With the toppling of the legally-elected government, an interim one was imposed. The country received a further set-back with the split in the PPP in 1955. "Ideological, racial and personal factors" were all associated with the split into 'Jaganite' and 'Burnhamite' factions of the party. This unfortunate development was to have serious repercussions later, and from which the country is yet to fully recover.

When the elective principle was restored in 1957, Jagan's PPP won the elections. The same year, Burnham's faction was renamed People's National Congress. At fresh elections in 1961, Jagan retained power. The colony was gripped with serious political and racial unrest between the turbulent 1962 and 1964 period with protest against the Kaldor Budget and the Labour Relationships Bills.

TOP (left to right): The Cabinet of the People's Progressive Party (PPP) Government in 1953, Ashton Chase (Labour and Commerce), Jainarine Singh (Local Government and Social Welfare), Cheddi Jagan (Premier, Agriculture, Forests, Lands and Mines), Janet Jagan (Deputy Speaker), Forbes Burnham (Education), Sydney King (Communications and Works), J.P. Lachmansingh (Health and Housing). BOTTOM (left to right): Arthur Chung was President for ten years from 1970. In 1980, a constitutional revision transformed the Presidency into an executive position; Forbes Burnham was Guyana's first Executive President from 1980 to 1985 (Photo: *Guyana Chronicle*); and Desmond Hoyte was President from 1985 to 1992.

In a very tense atmosphere, general elections were held in 1964 under a new system of proportional representation. The PPP won 24 seats, the PNC won 22 and the United Force obtained seven. With no party securing a majority, Forbes Burnham and the UF leader, industrialist Peter D'Aguiar, entered into a PNC/UF coalition and formed the government. The country achieved political independence on 26 May 1966 with Guyana as its name, and on 23 February 1970 it was proclaimed a Co-operative Republic. That year also marked the opening of the new premises of the University of Guyana at its Turkeyen Campus and the nationalisation of the Demerara Bauxite Company, a subsidiary of the Canadian-based Alcan. In 1975, Jessels Sugar Holding was nationalised. The nationalisation of Bookers Holdings followed in 1976.

In 1980, Prime Minister Burnham became Guyana's first Executive President following general elections under an extremely controversial new constitution. By the early 1980s, it was clear that the country was heading towards a serious economic crisis. The pillars of the economy – sugar, rice and bauxite – experienced declining production and fuel prices rose drastically. With a depletion in foreign currency reserves, shortage of raw materials and spares, and a rising national debt, living standards fell dramatically. Migration to neighbouring Suriname, Venezuela and Brazil, to the Caribbean and North America rose at an alarming rate.

In August 1985, President Burnham died at the Georgetown Hospital after undergoing surgery and Hugh Desmond Hoyte became his successor. In 1989, in the face of a worsening

Left to right: Cheddi Jagan was President from 1992 to 1997; Samuel Hinds was President in 1997 (Photo: *Guyana Chronicle*); and Janet Jagan was President from 1997 to 1999.

economic situation, the Hoyte administration embarked on an Economic Recovery Programme through agreement with the International Monetary Fund (IMF) and the Support Group of Countries. A massive devaluation that year led to shock, public outcry and strikes.

The early 1990s witnessed an intensification of the struggle for the restoration of democracy. In October 1992, under free and fair elections and internationally supervised, Dr Jagan made a triumphant return to office after a prolonged period in the political wilderness. He promptly embarked on the arduous task of nation-building. Unfortunately, Dr Jagan died in March 1997, a critical period in the overall recovery and rebuilding process.

The country was briefly administered by Samuel Hinds and following elections of December 1997, Mrs Janet Jagan was elected President. The immediate post-1997 period witnessed a wave of anti-government protests which were followed by CARICOM intervention, the Hermanston Accord and the St Lucia Agreement.

In 1999, Janet Jagan resigned the Presidency due to ill-health and she was succeeded by Bharrat Jagdeo. At the 2001 General Elections, the PPP/Civic was returned to office under the leadership of President Jagdeo.

Post-elections violence was followed by the emergence of the dialogue process with Desmond Hoyte in 2001. The following year, there was the Camp Street Prison jail-break and a subsequent increase in crimes including murder, robberies and kidnappings and the village of Buxton emerged as a haven for heightened criminal activity. Desmond Hoyte died the same year and Robert Corbin emerged as the Leader of the PNC/Reform.

A number of costly programmes were embarked upon. These include the East Demerara-West Berbice Highway, the Cheddi Jagan International Airport modernisation project, the Tain Berbice Campus, the Caricom Secretariat Headquarters, the Arthur Chung Conference Centre, the New Amsterdam Hospital, the Skeldon Modernisation and Expansion Project and the renovation or building of numerous schools and health centres. Progress has also been made in the rural potable water supply, electricity generation and the creation of several new housing settlements countrywide.

The PPP/Civic was returned to office at the 2006 general elections but it became a minority government under

Left to right: Bharrat Jagdeo was President from 1999 to 2011 and Donald Ramotar was President from 2011 to 2015 (Photos courtesy of the *Guyana Chronicle*)

David Granger became President of Guyana in May 2015 / MED

President Donald Ramotar at the subsequent 2011 elections which saw A Partnership of National Unity (APNU) – a combination of the PNC and a number of smaller parties, along with the newly emerged Alliance for Change (AFC) holding a one seat Majority in Parliament. The post 2011 period was rocked with political instability especially at the level of Parliament. There were also repeated allegations of lack of transparency and corruption on the part of the PPP administration. With mounting pressure and a stalemate at the Parliamentary level, President Ramotar was forced to abort his full tenure in office and call early elections in May 2015. The end result was a closely contested 2015 general elections at which the coalition of APNU-AFC prevailed with a plurality of votes and a one seat majority. The new government is headed by David Granger as President and the leader of the Opposition is Bharrat Jagdeo.

Guyana continues to face the daunting challenges of survival against the background of the harsh realities of globalisation. On the local front, the country has to intensify its efforts to ensure ongoing national progress and development, social and economic justice and national unity, as it celebrates its Golden Jubilee of Independence in 2016.

Tota C. Mangar, BA, MA, is a Senior Lecturer in History, former Deputy Vice Chancellor and former Acting Vice Chancellor at the University of Guyana and Project Co-ódinator of the Guyana Improving Teacher Education Project (GITEP)

Located on Main Street in Georgetown, State House is the official residence of the President of Guyana. Prior to Independence, it was the official residence of the Governors of British Guiana / IB

# *Our foremost political leaders and the nation*

Accomplished political leaders have a clear strategy for turning political visions into reality. Through well-honed analytical, political and emotional intelligence, these leaders chart paths to promising futures that include economic growth, material prosperity and human well-being. But in the best of times such leaders are rare and, in the developing world, extraordinarily scarce. Yet it is in these very developing countries, where public institutions are weak, greed and corruption strong, personal ambitions exaggerated and social expectations the highest, that good leaders are most needed. In these societies responsible leadership has the potential to effect the greatest change for good or for worse.

On the threshold of political emancipation, Guyana was blessed with leaders of generous political acumen. They understood the international political landscape, appreciated the power of the global imperial system, perceived its strengths, identified its weaknesses and shared a common vision to liberate their country.

In the early 1950s, a visiting Royal Commission was given cause to comment on the state of political maturity displayed by the leaders. They were deemed to be politically precocious and as a consequence Guyana won one of the more advanced constitutional forms around the Caribbean. Subsequently, and in spite of the 1953 constitutional setback, this notion of political maturity was reinforced in 1960 when, at the very first constitutional conference in London, Her Majesty's Government was persuaded to concede the principle of political independence.

The political turmoil which enveloped the country in the wake of the 1960 concession had its genesis in the American perception of the Caribbean Sea as its own particular sphere of influence and the perceived intrusion of Soviet Socialist influence in that area. To appreciate the circumstance which influenced the Kennedy Administration, it is necessary to remember that the US, since 1950, had appointed itself the leading exponent of the Cold War, aimed at containing the spread of communism beyond Eastern Europe.

Kennedy was particularly sensitive to the possible spread of communism into America's Caribbean and Latin American spheres of influence. The State Department was so committed to this American mission that it financed covert operations against leftist organisations across Latin America and facilitated the overthrow of the suspected leftist regime in Guatemala. Indeed, in 1953, the United States played a key role in the British ousting of the People's Progressive Party government after a mere 133 days in office.

America found it difficult to relate to the newly ensconced Castro regime which gained power in 1959, and by 1960 an already strained relationship was fractured when an aborted CIA sponsored invasion was repelled at the Bay of Pigs in Cuba. In 1962, the Washington administration discovered Soviet missiles based in Cuba, demanded their withdrawal and clamped an embargo on Cuba. The Kennedy Administration did not admit that Cuba was "unrecoverable" but were determined that Guyana would not become another socialist beachhead in the region.

While it seemed that Britain was still not explicitly opposed to independence for Guiana, American forces hostile to the idea worked assiduously to prevent it. In June 1963, President Kennedy stopped over in London on his way to Italy and conferred with Prime Minister Harold Macmillan. Drew Pearson, whose access to the most reliable sources on Capitol Hill made him the envy of the White House press corps, reported that under pressure from Kennedy, Macmillan agreed to defer independence to Guiana because of Cheddi Jagan's pro-communist ideology.

Recognising the agony of their betrayal, it has become almost fashionable for First World politicians to confess their manifold sins in Guyana and essay optimistic predictions as to the future of the country they fractured then discarded. Some have even attempted to promote the Guyana brand on the international investment market. The reality is that in spite of their initial intervention and the negative consequences of that intervention, Guyana must come to terms both with its potential and its future. Guyana's greatest potential is its people and its future can only reflect its potential if constructive bridges are built to unite the people. Guyana must become, One People, One Nation, One Destiny.

It is perhaps significant to note that on the occasion of Guyana's 34th Anniversary of Independence in 2000, distinguished American Democratic politician, Edolphus Towns Jr, paid glowing tribute to the memory and outstanding achievements of our Fathers of the Nation, Dr Cheddi Jagan and Mr Forbes Burnham, as well as to the government and people of Guyana. Mr Towns was at the time addressing the prestigious US House of Representatives of which he was a member for thirty years (1983-2013). He also served as Chairman of the House Oversight and Government Committee between the period 2009-2013. Congressional records on the admirable contribution of Mr Towns follow.

**HONORING THE HONORABLE LINDEN FORBES SAMPSON BURNHAM**
Hon. Edolphus Towns of New York
In the House of Representatives
*Tuesday, 16 May 2000*

Mr. Speaker, on this the 34th anniversary of the independence of Guyana, I rise to honor the memory and celebrate the achievements of the Honorable Linden Forbes Sampson Burnham, the former President of Guyana, and one of the most charismatic political personalities in the Caribbean region and in the Third World community. The Hon. Linden Forbes Sampson Burnham, like his contemporary and compatriot, Cheddie Jagan, enjoyed a political career that was unique and unparalleled.

Linden Forbes Sampson Burnham was born on February 20, 1923, in the village of Kitty, in the County of Demerara, in the nation of Guyana. He was the son of James Burnham, a Headmaster and Rachael Sampson, a housewife. From his parents, he inherited a profound love of learning and an intimate knowledge of the Bible.

Forbes Burnham was educated at Queens College in Guyana, London University and Gray's Inn in London, England. Upon his return from London, he embarked upon a political career that was nothing short of remarkable. He was a co-founder of the People's Progressive Party and was appointed Minister of Education in the first democratically elected government in Guyana. After the split with the People's Progressive Party, he founded the People's National Congress and became Leader of the Opposition in 1957. In 1966, he became Prime Minister of an independent Guyana and, in 1980, became the first President of the Republic of Guyana.

From his early years, Forbes Burnham had exhibited signs of academic brilliance. His keen intellect, sharp wit, photographic memory and awesome gift of public speaking, made Forbes Burnham a formidable political figure in Guyana, in the Caribbean and in the Third World. Forbes Burnham was in many respects a larger than life figure—a voracious reader of books, a passionate lover of the arts, a connoisseur of fine food, exotic wines and expensive cigars. He was in many respects the Caribbean Renaissance Man.

However, Forbes Burnham was more than a Renaissance Man. He was a Guyanese nationalist committed to the political and economic empowerment of his nation. He remained a dedicated advocate for the working class and remained President of the Guyana Labor Union for most of his career. He was a passionate supporter of Caribbean integration and Third World empowerment. Linden Forbes Sampson Burnham remains one of the most remarkable political personalities in the history of the Caribbean.

**HONORING THE HONORABLE. CHEDDIE B. JAGAN**
Hon. Edolphus Towns of New York
In the House of Representatives
*Tuesday, 16 May 2000*

Mr. Speaker, on this the 34th anniversary of the independence of Guyana, I rise to honor the memory and celebrate the achievements of the Hon. Cheddie B. Jagan, the former President of Guyana, and one of the most committed and dedicated political leaders in the Caribbean region and in the Third World community. Dr. Cheddie Jagan, like his contemporary and compatriot, Forbes Burnham, enjoyed a political career that can only be described as unique and unprecedented.

Cheddie B. Jagan was born on March 22, 1918, in the village of Port Mourant, in the County of Berbice, in the nation of Guyana. He was the son of Jagan and Bachoni, indentured plantation workers who had migrated from the state of Uttar Predesh in India. Dr. Jagan was to retain a profound commitment to the concerns of the rural sugar workers throughout his career.

Dr. Jagan was educated at Howard University and Northwestern University in the United States and returned to Guyana in 1946 to begin a remarkable political odyssey. In 1950, he founded the People's Progressive Party and, in April 1953, he headed the first democratically elected government in Guyana's history. In 1957, and again in 1961, he became Chief Minister of the Government. In 1964, he became a leader of the Parliamentary Opposition, and in October 1992, he was elected President of Guyana. On March 6, 1997, this monumental political figure passed away at the Walter Reed hospital in Washington, D.C.

Dr. Cheddie Jagan lived in a period of profound repression during the Cold War. Regrettably, the government of the United States played a significant role in destabilizing the government of Cheddie Jagan. In 1953, it persuaded the British Government to suspend the constitution; in 1955, it helped to split the national movement; and, in 1962, it helped to provoke civil disturbances. This tribute is a small attempt to atone for this gross miscarriage of justice.

Through all these political vicissitudes, Dr. Jagan maintained a constant and unwavering commitment to the cause of the Guyana working class, to the concept of working class unity and to the principles of constitutional democracy. In spite of overwhelming odds, Cheddie Jagan, like Dr. Martin Luther King, Jr., ultimately believed that "truth pressed to earth will rise again" and that "the arm of the moral universe is long, but it bends towards justice."

**A TRIBUTE TO THE NATION OF GUYANA**
Hon. Edolphus Towns of New York
In the House of Representatives
*Friday, 23 June 2000*

Mr. Speaker, on this the 34th anniversary of the independence of Guyana, I would like to pay tribute to the government and people of the extraordinary nation. Although this year marks the 34th anniversary of Guyana's independence, it would be misleading to assume that Guyana's sense of nationhood only began with the grant of independence 34 years ago.

Guyana's sense of nationhood existed over 500 years ago, among the Amerindian tribes that inhabited its tropical rainforest. It existed among the African warriors such as Kofi, Attah, Accabree, who launched their war of liberation in 1763. It existed among Indian indentured workers such as Rambarran, Pooran, Harry, and Surajballi who forfeited their lives in the struggle to improve working conditions on the sugar plantations.

Nationalism has existed in the literature of the Guyanese people. It has existed in the poetry of Martin Carter and Arthur Seymour; in the novels of Edgar Mittelholzer, Wilson Harris and Jan Carew; in the patriotic music of R.G.G. Potter, Valery Rodway, and Halley Bryant; in the rhythm of the Indian Tassa drums and the African bongos drums; and the call and response of the Guyanese folk songs.

Nature has been generous to the nation of Guyana. It has endowed her with an extensive network of over 40 rivers and creeks, and over 276 waterfalls, including Kaieteur Falls, which has a direct perpendicular drop of 741 feet. The land is richly endowed with natural resources—fertile agricultural lands; extensive savannahs; rich fishing and shrimping grounds; over 500 species of tropical hardwoods including greenheart, mora, baromalli, purpleheart, and crabwood, and a wide variety of minerals including gold, diamonds, bauxite, manganese, titanium, columbite/tantalite, copper and nickel.

In spite of its rich history of struggle and extensive natural resources, Guyana faces formidable political, social and economic problems. In the 1950s, Guyana had one of the most progressive movements in the Caribbean, based upon the principles of Guyanese nationalism and socialism. However, in 1955 the political movement split, ushering in two decades of racial antagonism. Racial divisions have stymied economic development, creating an environment of instability and uncertainty. In spite of an impressive growth rate during the last decade, Guyana still remains one of the poorest and least developed nations in the Western hemisphere.

The Guyanese people are a resourceful, gifted and resilient people who are capable of confronting and overcoming the formidable problems that confront them. The historian Rodway described agricultural cultivation in Guyana as a daily struggle with the sea in front and the flood behind. The historian Walter Rodney has noted how the African slaves built the sugar plantations by moving "one hundred million tons of heavy water-logged clay with shovel in hand, while enduring conditions of perpetual water and mud." The historian Eusi Kaywana has noted that the Berbice rebellion of 1763 predated the American Revolution of 1776, the French Revolution of 1789, the French Revolution of 1791, the Paris commune of 1848 and the Russian Revolution of 1917.

Ironically, the policy of the U.S. government has been one of suspicion and hostility towards the governments of Guyana. We conspired with the British in 1960 to suspend the constitution, and to destabilize the government of Cheddie Jagan between 1957 and 1964. When President Burnham implemented socialist policies in the 1970s, we discouraged U.S. foreign investment, bilateral aid and multilateral loans to Guyana.

It is time for the U.S. government to change its policy towards the nation of Guyana. Guyana has become an attractive location for foreign investment. There is a stable political environment that is committed to private enterprise; there is a system of Parliamentary democracy with free elections and an independent Judiciary; there is a substantial natural resource base; there has been radical and substantial economic growth over the last decade; there is preferential access to the Caribbean, Latin America, North America and European markets; there is a skilled and trainable labor force proficient in the English language. Guyana is an investment opportunity whose time has come.

More than half of Guyana's population is Christian, and attending church on Sunday is a revered family occasion / IB

## A land of many peoples

Today's Guyanese have descended from six groups from six of the world's continents, five of whom settled since 1492. The first group of settlers, from several indigenous nations, arrived from Mongolia via North and Central America. The Europeans came from Holland, Portugal, Britain, France and Spain in search of El Dorado the mythical city of gold. Later the Dutch and British colonisers were to bring enslaved Africans to work on the sugar plantations followed by indentured Portuguese, Indian and Chinese labourers.

Guyana has a diverse heritage that is a rich blend of history, beliefs and traditions that are drawn from the descendants of many nations.

It is truly a "Land of Many Peoples."

### THE FIRST PEOPLES
*Dr Desrey C. Fox*

The indigenous peoples of Guyana are the descendants of the first settlers who lived in the region approximately 12,000 years prior to the arrival of the first European settlers in 1492. In those early days, there were many nations – Trios, Tarumas, Miyonggongs, Piyanogottos, Atorads, Taurepang and Kamarakoto among others.

Many of these groups became extinct or fled from the region for a number of reasons such as illnesses, inter-tribal wars and forced migration by European missionaries. Several left because they resented colonial rule that allowed 'free

Residents of Paramakatoi in the central region of Potaro-Siparuni (Region 8). Located near Guyana's western border with Brazil, the community is the largest and most developed indigenous community in the region / KJ

Guyana's indigenous population stands at about 70,000 / IB

nation' status to some and categorised others as 'slaves'.

These 'free nations' were the Arawaks, Akawaios, Caribs and Warraus.

The population of indigenous peoples is approximately 70,000; a figure difficult to verify because members of the various communities travel frequently between neighbouring countries and also create satellite communities both close to and far from established villages.

The indigenous peoples of Guyana can be categorised linguistically and anthropologically into three main human and language groups: Arawakan, Cariban and Warrauan. Each of these nations has its own language and each is defined linguistically by the same categories. They also occupy relatively well-defined separate ecological niches that have influenced their distinct cultures.

Guyana has some of the most educated indigenous peoples in the region and many now leave their communities to pursue higher education at the University of Guyana and Cyril Potter College of Education. In addition, the Hinterland Scholarship, initiated by the government, provides the opportunity for the children of indigenous Guyanese to attend some of the top secondary schools in Georgetown.

The presence of the country's first peoples has been the longest in Guyana and, therefore, as indigenous peoples, they have helped to forge a nation out of an untamed land to create the foundation of what is now Guyana. As the communities interact more and more with other cultures they will redefine themselves and find new roles in this multicultural and pluralistic society.

*Editor's footnote. It is with regret that we acknowledge the passing of Desrey Fox. The quality of this article, which appeared in the second edition of* Guyana, *inspired us to reprint it here.*

Young Guyanese enjoying the Buxton/Foulis Mash parade / MED

Vendors at Bourda market in Georgetown / IB

# THE AFRICAN GUYANESE
*Christobel Hughes*

The presence of Africans in Guyana begins in the first half of the seventeenth century when a Charter was issued to the Dutch West India Company in 1621 to supply workers from Africa. However, it was not until 1665-6, after the expulsion of the Dutch from Brazil, that the Dutch West India Company threw open the Guiana coast by inviting settlers to inhabit the area (with their slaves) on condition that they purchased their supplies from, and traded their produce in, Zeeland, a western province of The Netherlands.

The African presence in Guyana can be defined by its involvement in the sugar industry and the contributions that African people have made towards the overall development of the colony and, ultimately, Guyana as a nation. Africans had driven back the sea and cleared, drained and reclaimed some 15,000 miles of swamp and forest. In short, all the fields on which the sugar estates are now based were cleared, drained and irrigated by slave labour before 1834 and African slave labour moved millions of tons of clay, with only shovels and bare hands, to build the coastal plantations. The so-called 'Wilde Coast' was tamed and humanised by the African worker.

The period following Emancipation (1838 to 1853) has been described as one of the most remarkable in Guyanese history. The former slaves, who desired nothing more than to quit the estates, were able to accumulate funds earned during apprenticeship to purchase abandoned estates. This period saw the establishment of 'co-operative villages'. Northbrook (later re-named Victoria) was acquired in 1839 and became the first co-operative village.

The outcome of the African labour strikes in 1842 and 1847 gave impetus to further land purchases on the part of the former slaves although on a smaller scale. The strikes also intensified the planters' efforts to prevent the

Officers of the City Constabulary patrolling the streets of Georgetown / MED

Fishing from a footbridge / IB

An officer of the Guyana Fire Service attending a blaze in Georgetown / KJ

former slaves, particularly those with the necessary financial power, from squatting on Crown lands or moving to the interior.

In the sixty years after slavery was abolished, it was a battle for economic survival and self-preservation. Despite all the obstacles and lack of credit, the Africans found outlets for their creativity. They grasped education and became the professionals, teachers, village leaders, nurses, civil servants, doctors, lawyers and ministers of religion. They pioneered the mining and forest industries and agitated for reform of the political system.

Despite the centuries of subjugation and humiliation, the Guyanese African continues to make significant contributions to life in Guyana.

*Editor's footnote. It is with regret that we acknowledge the passing of Christobel Hughes. The quality of this article, which appeared in the second edition of* Guyana, *inspired us to*

# THE INDIAN GUYANESE
*Tota C. Mangar*

For over three quarters of a century labourers were exported from India to the West Indian colonies ostensibly to fill the void created by the mass exodus of African labourers from the plantations following the abolition of slavery and, more so, the premature termination of the apprenticeship scheme in 1838.

This influx was only one segment of a wider movement of Indian labour to other parts of the world and Guyana (formerly British Guiana) was the recipient of 239,909 Indian immigrants up to 1917.

The importation of labourers from India, the 'Gladstone Experiment', was part of the continuing search for a reliable labour force to meet the needs of the powerful plantocracy. John Gladstone (father of British liberal statesman William Gladstone) was the proprietor of two West Demerara estates – Vreed-en-Hoop and

A barber takes care of his young customer / IB

On a farm in Berbice / IB

planters were beginning to experience an acute labour shortage as a consequence of the mass withdrawal of African labour from the plantations. Gladstone wrote to the Calcutta recruiting firm, Gillanders, Arbutnot and Company, enquiring about the possibility of obtaining Indian immigrants for his estates. The firm's prompt reply was that it envisaged no recruiting problems and that Indians were already in service in another British colony, Mauritius. Subsequently, Gladstone received permission for his 'experiment' from both the Colonial Office and the Board of Control of the East India Company.

The first group of Indian labourers arrived in Guyana on board the steamships 'Whitby' and 'Hesperus' on 5th May 1838.

This 'experiment' was not confined to Gladstone's two estates but included the plantations of Highbury and Waterloo in Berbice, Bell View in West Bank Demerara and Anna Regina on the Essequibo coast.

Since their arrival in British Guiana in 1838, Indian labourers have played a significant role in the survival of the sugar industry right up to the twenty-first century and are also largely responsible for the prominence of Guyana's rice industry. They cultivated rice on a large scale and this was linked to the most exclusive Indian village settlements which emerged at the time. They were also integrally involved in cattle-rearing, milk-selling and cash crop cultivation.

Ever since the 1880s, Indian labourers and their descendants have displayed high occupational profiles in a number of off-plantation activities including cab drivers, barbers, tailors, carpenters, boat-builders, charcoal-makers, goldsmiths, porters, small-scale manufacturers and fishermen.

Today, Guyanese of Indian origin are found in every sphere of activity including business, the professional class, politics and trade unions and has made and continue to make invaluable contributions to the overall progress and development of Guyana. They have ensured that there is a rich cultural heritage in the multi-cultural and pluralistic society that is Guyana.

# THE PORTUGUESE GUYANESE
*Mary Noel Menezes*

On 3rd May 1835, the ship 'Louisa Baillie' docked in Demerara with forty immigrants from Madeira on board, bound for work on British Guiana's sugar plantations. They came in response to the approaching abolition of slavery and subsequent labour shortages.

However, by 1845, most of the Portuguese had moved off the plantations and had bought small plots of land and moved into the huckster and retail trades.

In the early years, it was mainly in the rum trade that the Portuguese made their mark. By 1852, more than three quarters of the country's retail rum shops were owned by the Portuguese and they retained that monopoly well into the twentieth century. The end of the 1860s and the 1870s saw the Portuguese well entrenched in the business community. Apart from being property owners, they were merchants, shop owners, importers, iron mongers, ship chandlers, leather merchants, boot and shoe makers, saddlers, coach-builders, timber merchants, brick makers, cattle owners, pork-knockers, charcoal dealers, bakers and photographers.

In 1858, the number of Portuguese in British Guiana was approximately 35,000, of which almost all were Catholic. They brought not only their agricultural expertise but their faith as well, bolstered by the arrival of Portuguese-speaking priests.

In 1861, they built the Sacred Heart Church in Georgetown as well as other churches along the East Coast and East Bank, in Demerara and Essequibo. Of all the religious customs brought over by the Portuguese, the Christmas Novena continues to hold sway among Catholic Guyanese of every ethnic origin.

The Portuguese held on to their language throughout the nineteenth century and a number of Portuguese newspapers kept the community in touch with events in Madeira and in the colony. Portuguese schools were established and together with other amateur and professional groups, the Portuguese contributed to the developing cultural stream of music and drama in British Guiana society.

The Portuguese were also prominent in the world of sports – boxing, cricket, cycling, rugby, football, tennis, hockey, racing and rowing. In 1898, the Portuguese formed the first cycling club, The Vasco da Gama Cycling Club. In 1952, the Portuguese Club was founded and nurtured several famous tennis players of the day.

However much the Portuguese added to the cultural dimension, their entry into the political field took much longer. First, there was the language barrier; secondly, the majority of the Portuguese men were not naturalised British subjects and thirdly, the government constantly cautioned the Portuguese "not to meddle with politics" but to stick to their business. Not until 1906 did any member from the Portuguese community run for office, with F.I. Dias and J.P. Santos winning seats in the Court of Policy and Combined Court.

However, although the Portuguese had gained a political foothold, they were not at all welcomed with open arms into the colonial government.

By the turn of the century, the Portuguese had created their own middle and upper classes but they were never accepted into the echelons of white European society, even though they were European. The rapid economic progress of the Portuguese, their strong adherence to the Catholic faith and their clannishness bred respect but never whole-hearted acceptance among the population in either the nineteenth or twentieth centuries.

In the 1960s and 1970s, the Portuguese suffered even more discrimination and many left Guyana in search of greener pastures.

# THE CHINESE GUYANESE
*Marjorie Kirkpatrick*

The Chinese came to British Guiana as indentured labourers between 1853 and 1879. They brought with them their love of food and culinary skills; so much so that Chinese restaurants can be found on almost every block in the capital and in most country districts. Through their culinary expertise they transformed local foods found in Guyana with Chinese flavourings, preparations and substitute ingredients.

In the case of the 'Chinee cake', the original was the Chinese bean cake, 'towsa peng', but with its local incarnation it was made with black-eyed peas. They made 'ham choy (preserved greens) with the local mustard plant that they grew here and 'salted egg' with the local duck eggs, to replace the 'hundred-year egg'.

Over the years, the Chinese have stamped their presence firmly on Guyanese society in many ways. Such as The St Saviour's Parish

Since the mid-nineteenth century, the Chinese community has made a significant contribution to Guyanese society / KJ

Smile, and the whole world smiles with you / KJ

Traditional Indian dance / KJ

Chinese-Guyanese have made their mark throughout Guyanese society / KJ

Church, originally known as the 'Chinese Church', when it was consecrated in 1874, as part of the parish of St Phillip's in Georgetown.

Or through the Chinese Sports Club, which became the Cosmos Sports Club, and later acquired by the Guyana Motor Racing Club, and where children of Chinese heritage excelled at lawn tennis and table tennis giving Guyana the West Indies Championship on several occasions. Hockey was another popular sport and in the 1960s and 70s the National Team was made up almost entirely of players of Chinese origin.

Members of Guyana's Chinese community were able to make their mark as scholars, teachers, university professors, lawyers, doctors, dentists, farmers, shopkeepers, business leaders and political leaders.

The only Chinese customs that have withstood the test of time are practiced by individual families: wedding customs, the hospitality of the people and the celebration of any event whatsoever, by a feast of Chinese foods. However, with the arrival of newcomers from China, aspects of Chinese culture and traditions are given a new lease of life; the Spring Festival (the Chinese New Year) complete with lion dance and festive dinner is now a must on the country's festival timetable.

This has raised the consciousness of those of Chinese ancestry and allowed other Guyanese to appreciate aspects of Chinese culture that had slipped away over time.

This young man hopes that his prized finch will chirp or whistle the loudest or longest in the local 'bird racing' competition / IB

A Mash parade through the village of Buxton / MED

Laughter really is the best medicine / KJ

Fresh coconut water vendors are a common sight on the busy streets of Guyana / IB

A popular food-stop outside Stabroek Market in Georgetown / KA

A school trip in Georgetown / IB

Sweetie-stop at a local convenience store in Leguan / KA

Gathering lotus lily leaves for a Hindu wedding ceremony. Known locally as 'puri leaf' or 'kamalgatta', the leaves are used like plates upon which food is served / IB

Popular Georgetown vendor selling his leather goods from the bonnet of his prized Toyota motor car / IB

Road-side sugarcane juice / IB

Sluice gates or kokers, as they are known locally, protect the low-lying areas from high tides / IB

## So much to see, so much to do

So you've arrived at the Cheddi Jagan International Airport and you're wondering what you're going to be doing during your stay in Guyana. There is so much that's ahead of you...so much to see and do. You'll leave the airport in one of the taxis or minibuses and head down the east bank road towards the capital city of Georgetown. The road runs along the banks of the Demerara River and for the most part is bordered by vegetation. It's a scenic ride and along the route you'll begin to get a taste of the wooden architecture that's still the predominant style used for the construction of houses in this country that boasts one of the largest tropical forests left in the world.

The journey will eventually bring you to the Diamond Sugar estate, home of the world famous El Dorado Rums, and then it will be on into the city. You might want to stop at the Ramada Princess Hotel and Casino, if that's to your liking, or head on in to central Georgetown.

Maybe you should ask the driver to take you past the Parliament Buildings, Law Courts and City Hall, all iconic buildings that sit along the Avenue of the Republic, one of the city's main thoroughfares. If you continue along this route you'll get a glimpse of the Non-aligned Monument and the world's tallest one-storey wooden building, the beautiful gothic St. George's Cathedral. The National Library and the country's central bank also occupy this intersection.

What an arrival, you've just been given a front seat view of the sites that make any visit to Georgetown special.

Continuing down this route along Main Street will take you past State House, the official residence of the country's President, and just a little further down, the Prime Minister's Residence, both wooden buildings that have been painstakingly restored to showcase the colonial architectural style in which they were built. And then it's on into Kingston, where you'll encounter, Red House, the home of Guyana's first Premier and former President, Dr. Cheddi Jagan and across the road, Austin House, the residence of the Anglican Archbishop of the Caribbean.

The Pegasus and Marriott Hotels both overlook the seawall and Atlantic Ocean and are

Toll booths on the Demerara Harbour Bridge / IB

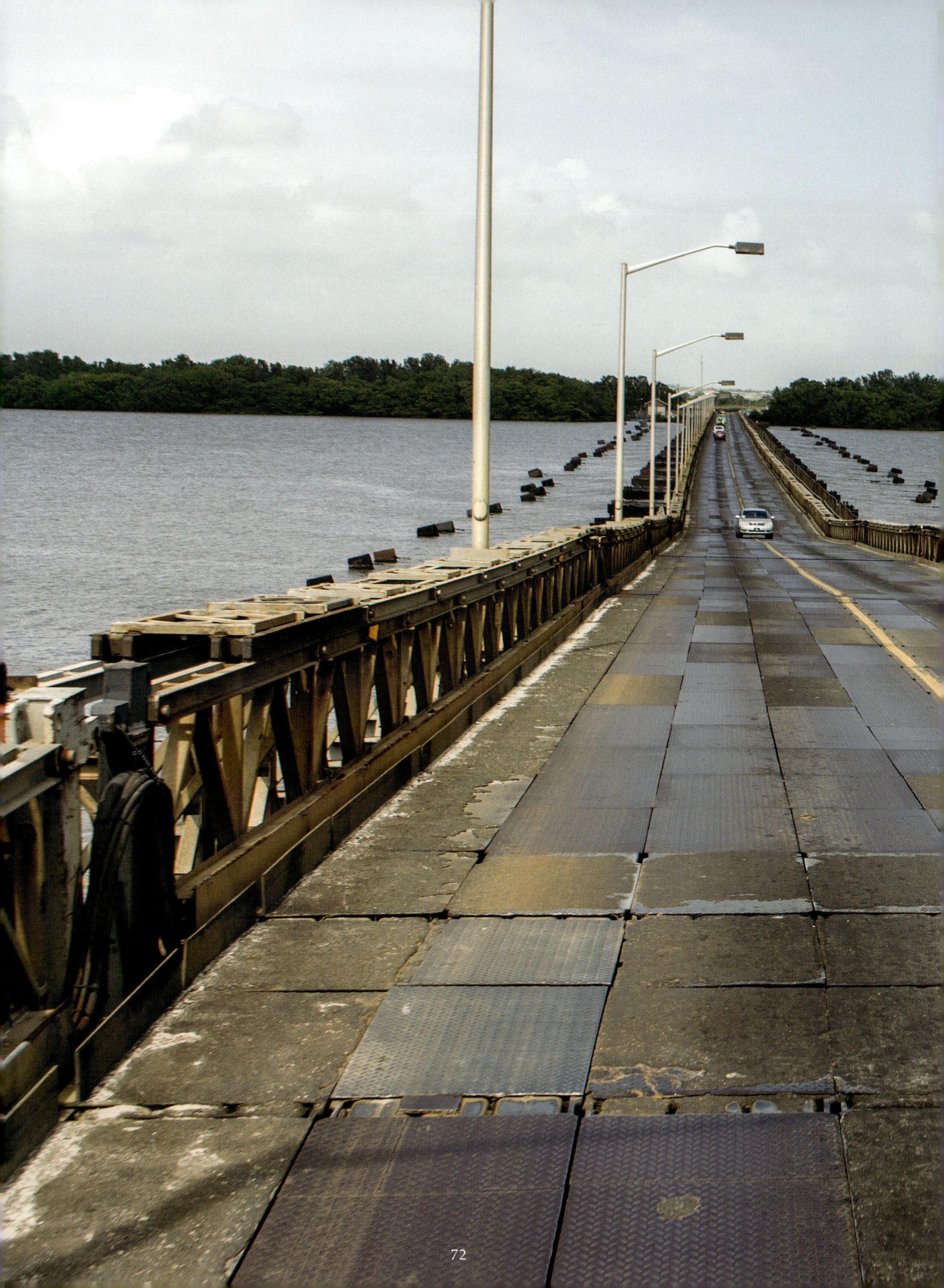

The Demerara Harbour Bridge is a floating toll bridge that was opened in 1978. As its name suggests, the bridge crosses the Demerara River four miles south of the capital. A raised section allows small vessels to pass under it and a retractor span allows large vessels to pass through it. The bridge was designed and built to last ten years but, nearly four decades on, it is still providing a vital transport link between West Coast Demerara and Georgetown / IB

The Rupununi River flows through south-western Guyana in the Upper Takutu-Upper Essequibo region (Region 9). It is one of the main tributaries of the Essequibo River / GTA

at the end of this route along Main Street. But if you look to the skies you may see several colourful kites dancing in the tropical breezes. But the building to really feast your eyes on is the recently rebuilt Umana Yana, a troolie thatched wooden structure that was built by the Wai Wai indigenous nation in their traditional style in 1972 for the non-aligned Foreign Ministers' Conference. Umana Yana means "meeting place of the people."

There is much to do in the city; restaurants galore offering both gourmet dining and fast foods; several watering holes dispensing beer and spirits to slake any thirsts and a night time economy to rival any other Caribbean city.

You can choose from a smorgasbord of epicurean delights of Creole, Chinese, Indian, Amerindian, Rastafarian and Mediterranean cuisine that will titillate your palate and leave you longing for more. The New Thriving Restaurant on Main Street offers some of the best in Caribbean Chinese cuisine; The Oasis on Carmichael Street is a coffee shop and Restaurant that mixes local and Mediterranean styles; there is the Palm Court, Midtown Café Shanta's for Indian fare and sweetmeats Maggie's and the ubiquitous fast food restaurants.

Church's Chicken, Quiznos, Mario's Pizzeria and Bruster's Ice Cream are all within walking distance of the city centre and then there are those on the outskirts – Buddy's Mei Tung Chinese Restaurant, Aagman Indian Restaurant that sit along Sheriff Street, where numerous night spots offer endless entertainment and makes this the street that never sleeps.

After dinner, there is the cinema, nightclubs theatre, and of course, in a country that produces some of the best liquors in the world, the rum shops that provide one of the popular forms of evening entertainment for the adult population

Next morning, take things light and visit the National Museum in Georgetown, a private museum on the west coast of Demerara at Meten-Meer-Zorg or the one in Linden. You are spoilt for choice as both the Police Academy and Guyana Defence Force have museums chronicling their history. Castellani House, the

The Potaro-Siparuni region (Region 8) borders northern Brazil / KJ

Built in 1743 during the Dutch colonial era, Fort Zeelandia is situated on Fort Island at the mouth of the Essequibo River. It was a vital defence fortification and was built to withstand the heaviest bombardment / IB

Promenade Gardens in Georgetown / IB

former residence of the first Executive President, Forbes Burnham, houses the national art collection. These are open to the public, so take some time to visit.

The people of Georgetown are multi-lingual and if you get lost and need to ask directions you may well be answered in English or Creolese.

Guyana proudly defines its national identity as South American and Amazonian and the country is the gateway to undiscovered areas of the continent. Leaving the city, you can undertake journeys up spectacular black water creeks and rivers; witness ancient cultures practised by peoples proud of their origins and experience the natural beauty of the country.

You can do so in several ways; there are a myriad of tours and opportunities for the adventurous traveller.

You can take an outing to one of the creeks. Guyana's creeks feature 'black water', a phenomenon thought to be the result of staining from the numerous trees that border these waterways. Their white sand beaches are in direct contrast to the dark mahogany coloured water

water and eat labba, a large rodent found in tropical and sub-tropical America, you are destined to return to Guyana.

Nature lovers must not leave these shores without a visit to the magnificent Kaieteur Falls the world's tallest one-drop falls, tumbling some 741 feet down the gorge. A sight to behold spectacular and quite probably the only location of the rare golden frog.

Using the country's navigable waters, you can also enjoy river tours to places of historic interest and sightseeing of unique flora and fauna. Journeying up the Mahaica River, for example, will take you past Victoria, the first village purchased by the freed slaves and you will glimpse the Hoatzin, Guyana's national bird known locally as the Canje Pheasant.

The country is home to the jaguar, its national animal; the arapaima, the world's largest fresh water fish, a bird-watcher's dream with species that are found nowhere else on earth, hot springs at Mainstay on the Essequibo coast, yachting in the Essequibo River, otters at Karanambo Ranch in the Rupununi, Rodeo in the Rupununi and Regatta at Bartica during

Schoolchildren in Paramakatoi in Potaro-Siparuni (Region 8). The community is the largest and most developed indigenous community in the region / KJ

The ward of West Ruimveldt in Georgetown / IB

La Penitence market in Georgetown / KJ

Lumber merchant in Campbellville, Georgetown / IB

Parika Market / KA

Newspapers are sold in all locations and by all ages / KJ

The comfort of a guiding hand / IB

The interior is also dotted with eco-tourism resorts so you'll have no problem finding one that fits your particular requirements. The choices are endless and there is something for everyone.

Paved roads along the coast and into the interior now make trips to outlying communities relatively simple and you can easily travel along the length of the coast from Anna Regina in the west to Moleson Creek in the east. It is only at the Essequibo River that you will have to take a ferry since both the Demerara and Berbice rivers are can now be crossed by floating bridges. In fact, the Berbice bridge is the 6th longest floating bridge (1,57km) in the world!

Travelling south will take you to the mining town of Linden, Kwakwani and eventually to Lethem, the town that sits on the border with Brazil. From Lethem, you can enter the town of Bonfim in Brazil via the Takutu River Bridge. hat journey is best taken in the dry season however, when the roads are more navigable. The Brazil-Guyana road is now largely complete and so movement between the two countries has increased significantly.

Don't leave Guyana without taking a speedboat ride up one of the numerous waterways: there are many national monument sites outside of the capital. Try, if you can, to visit Kyk-Over-Al, one of the earliest Dutch settlements, which sits at the confluence of the Potaro and Mazaruni rivers, or Fort Nassau up the Berbice River, another Dutch outpost that was razed during the 1763 Rebellion.

The history of Guyana is replete with evidence of the many groups that populated these shores. This can be most readily seen in the place names that now dot our map. Make it your duty to soak up the beauty of this land.

*Russel Lancaster*

Transporting timber by horse cart / IB

Guyana has vast forest resources that cover more than three-quarters of its landmass and contain over 1,000 different tree varieties. Currently, 120 species are being logged in various forms, with between 12 and 15 of these logged on a commercial scale / IB

Fishing is a popular and widespread activity among the young / KJ

Kokers, or sluice gates, are strategically located along Guyana's coastal plain to protect the low-lying areas from high tides. These structures, and the canals, are a legacy of the Dutch colonial era and still provide protection and a vital transportation network / IB

The Moruca River is in Region 1 (Barima-Waini) in northern Guyana. A number of settlements are located along the river including Kamwatta Hill, Asakata and Santa Rosa, which is home to the country's largest indigenous Guyanese community / GTA

Entrance to Vreed-en-Hoop ferry stelling / IB

The mid-morning ferry to Leguan Island / KA

The waters throughout Guyana are an angler's delight / GTA

Arrival at Leguan Island ferry stelling / KA

Dining area at Giftland Mall in Georgetown / IB

Road-side vendor selling homemade delights / IB

Culinary essentials offered alongside medicinal potions at Georgetown's vibrant Bourda Market / IB

Rupununi in the south-west region of Upper Takutu-Upper Essequibo is populated by mainly indigenous Guyanese / IB

Guyana Police Force recruits / IB

Holy Redeemer Anglican Church in West Ruimveldt, Georgetown / IB

Mosque in Moleson Creek on the Corentyne River in East Berbice-Corentyne (Region 6) / IB

Novar Sri Krishna Mandir (temple) in Berbice / IB

St Peter's Anglican Church in Leguan / KA

Hindu temple in Berbice / IB

Church of the Transfiguration in La Penitence, Greater Georgetown / IB

Georgetown in Pictures

The Centotaph in Georgetown was unveiled in 1923 as a memorial to the Guyanese who died during the First World War, and then the Second World War. It stands against the backdrop of St George's Cathedral and is a poignant reminder of the nation's fallen soldiers / IB

# Georgetown in Pictures

Established in 1882, the striking clock tower and wooden facade of Kitty Market has been a distinct landmark in Greater Georgetown for more than 130 years. The timber-framed structure was home to vendors serving the Atlantic coast neighbourhoods in the east end of the city. In 2016, after many years of deterioration, a programme of repairs and renovation was commenced / KJ

Traditional street-sellers and 21st century commerce ply their trade side-by-side in the busy streets of Guyana's capital / IB

After Stabroek and Bourda, La Penitence market is another busy centre for a wide variety of produce / KJ

Georgetown in Pictures

Stabroek Market in the capital is Guyana's biggest market. Completed in 1881, the iron and steel clocktower and covered building reflect the architecture of Britain's Victorian era / KA

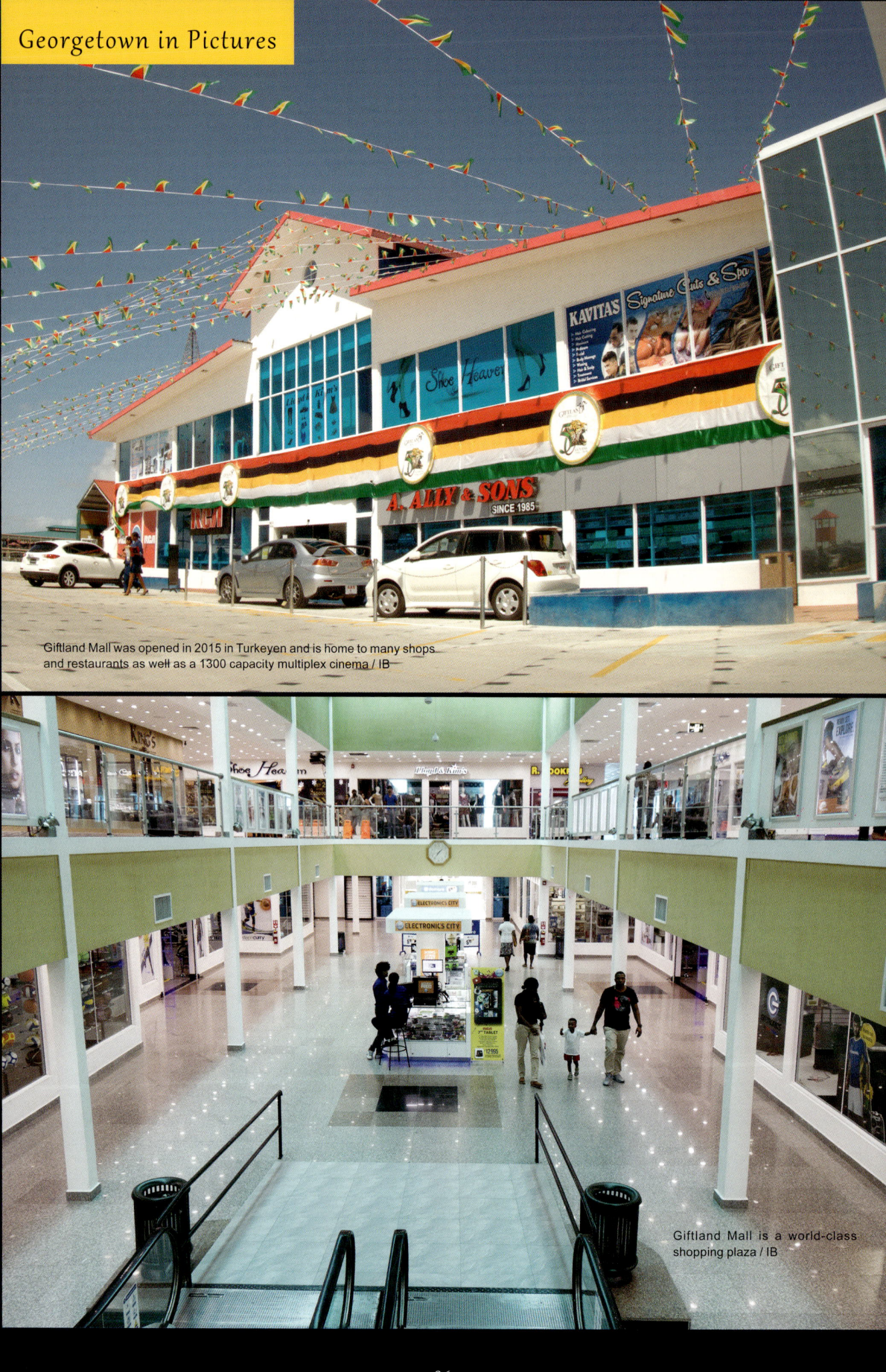

# Georgetown in Pictures

Giftland Mall was opened in 2015 in Turkeyen and is home to many shops and restaurants as well as a 1300 capacity multiplex cinema / IB

Giftland Mall is a world-class shopping plaza / IB

City Hall is a nineteenth-century Gothic Revival building located in the capital. It was completed in 1889 and is home to the Mayor of Georgetown, the City Council and the City Engineer. It is one of Guyana's National Monuments and is often described as the most picturesque building in Georgetown as well as being one of the finest examples of Gothic architecture in the Caribbean / IB

# Georgetown in Pictures

Bourda Market was first established in 1880 when vendors were relocated from Stabroek Market while it was being rebuilt. Stallholders chose to remain in the area after developing strong relationships with their customers / IB

Vendors at the Hibiscus Craft Plaza offer a wide range of handmade items and souvenirs / IB

St George's Anglican Cathedral dominates the centre of Georgetown and is one of the world's tallest wooden structures, standing at 143 ft. The building was completed in 1899 and is the seat of the Bishop of Guyana. It has been designated a National Monument / KJ

# Georgetown in Pictures

Brickdam Cathedral is the leading Catholic church in Guyana. It was opened in 1921 and is formally known as the Cathedral of Immaculate Conception / IB

Like any other capital city across the world, Georgetown serves as a hub for administrative, retail and financial services / KA

The Georgetown Lighthouse was first built by the Dutch in 1817, and then rebuilt in 1830, to help guide ships into the Demerara River from the Atlantic Ocean. The octagonal structure is a famous Guyanese landmark and is an official National Monument / IB

# Georgetown in Pictures

The 1763 Monument is situated in the Square of the Revolution in Georgetown and depicts Kofi Badu, or 'Cuffy' as he is popularly known. Cuffy led a revolt by more than three thousand slaves against the Dutch colonial powers in 1763. The statue was erected in 1976 and unveiled by Guyana's then Prime Minster, Forbes Burnham. Cuffy is acknowledged as one of Guyana's national heroes / IB

Since the 1980s, Guyana Stores has been a significant feature of the Georgetown shopping experience / IB

City Mall is located at the corner of Camp and Regent Streets in the busy heart of the capital. More than seventy shops are housed within this modern, fully air-conditioned environment. / IB

# Georgetown in Pictures

Austin House is the home of the Anglican Bishop of Guyana. Originally contructed in 1842, and rebuilt in 1894, it is a typical example of colonial architecture with its Georgian windows and Demerara shutters / IB

The headquarters of the Caribbean Community (Caricom) Secretariat commenced operations in 2006. This impressive building is located at Turkeyen in Greater Georgetown / IB

The Wakili Totem Pole was errrected in the National Park in 2015 and is made from purpleheart wood. The 20-foot pole was carved by Lokono (Arawak) artist, Oswald 'Ossie' Hussein and tells the ancient story of man's abiding respect for the forest and all it provides / IB

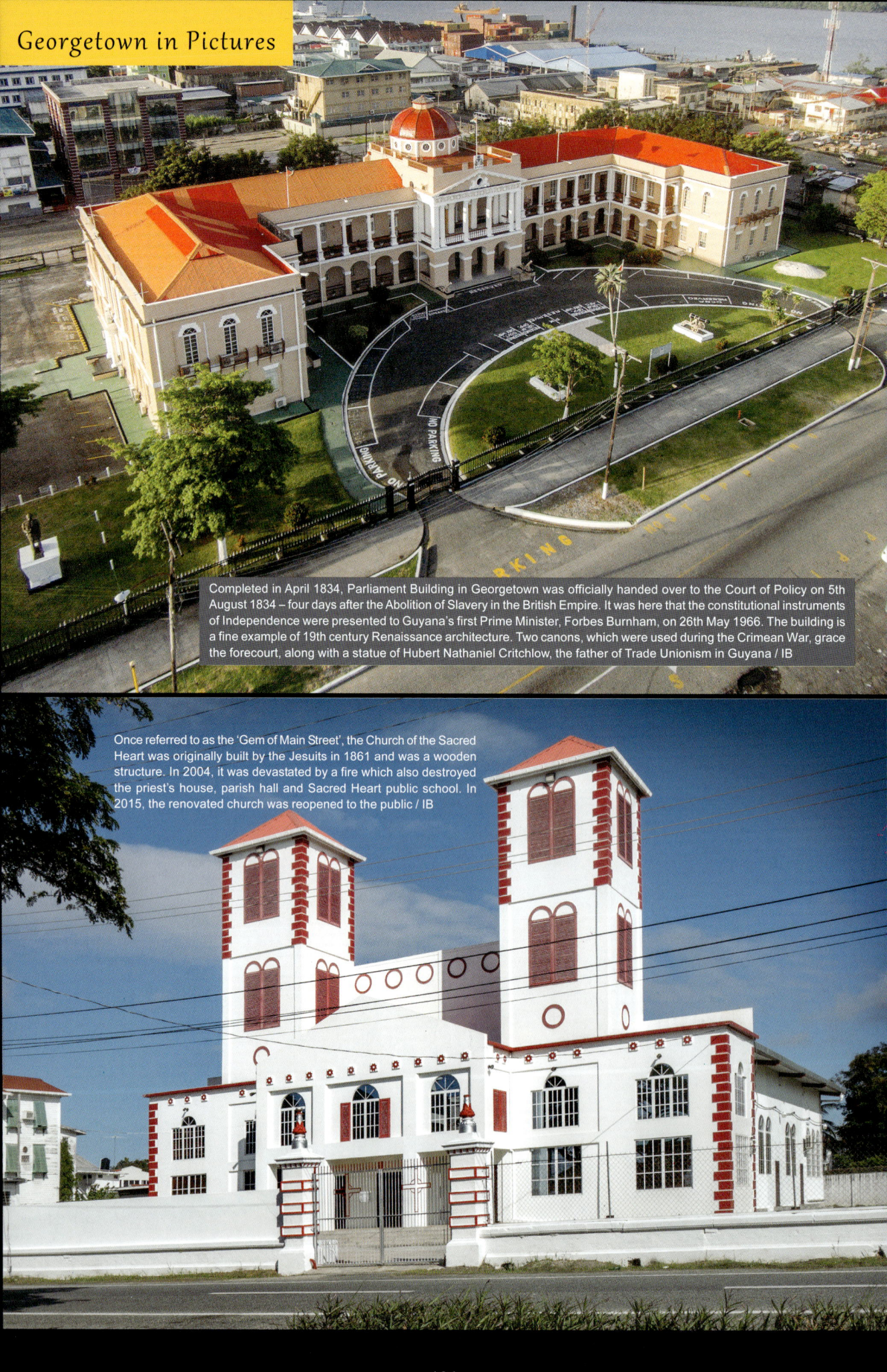

# Georgetown in Pictures

Completed in April 1834, Parliament Building in Georgetown was officially handed over to the Court of Policy on 5th August 1834 – four days after the Abolition of Slavery in the British Empire. It was here that the constitutional instruments of Independence were presented to Guyana's first Prime Minister, Forbes Burnham, on 26th May 1966. The building is a fine example of 19th century Renaissance architecture. Two canons, which were used during the Crimean War, grace the forecourt, along with a statue of Hubert Nathaniel Critchlow, the father of Trade Unionism in Guyana / IB

Once referred to as the 'Gem of Main Street', the Church of the Sacred Heart was originally built by the Jesuits in 1861 and was a wooden structure. In 2004, it was devastated by a fire which also destroyed the priest's house, parish hall and Sacred Heart public school. In 2015, the renovated church was reopened to the public / IB

Located along the Kitty sea wall on Carifesta Avenue, the 1823 Slave Revolt monument commemorates the Demerara rebellion by more than 10,000 slaves / IB

Georgetown in Pictures

Guyana's Sea Wall runs for 280 miles along much of the country's Atlantic coastline, including all of the coastline of the capital. Construction began in 1855 using primarily convict labour and it was completed in 1892. The wall protects the many coastal settlements that are below sea level at high tide. In Georgetown, the Sea Wall is a popular venue, particulary on Sundays, for family picnics, musicians, cyclists, kite-flying and siteseers / IB

Georgetown in Pictures

High tide often attracts spectators to the Sea Wall / IB

# Georgetown in Pictures

The closing stages of the renovation of the Umana Yana provide a rare opportunity to see the scale and construction techniques of this iconic building. In 2014, the palm-thatched benab was destroyed by fire. It was rebuilt in 2016 / IB

Built in 1972 for the Non-Aligned Foreign Ministers' Conference held in Georgetown, the Umana Yana is a palm-thatched hut (benab) which is used as an exhibition and conference centre. It was destroyed by fire in 2014 and rebuilt in 2016. Umana Yana is a Wai-Wai word meaning 'meeting place of the people' / IB

Established in the late 19th century, Georgetown's Botanical Gardens are among the finest tropical gardens in the Caribbean. The grounds are home to one of the most extensive collections of tropical flora in the region and are laid out with ponds, canals, kissing bridges and a bandstand / IB

# Georgetown in Pictures

Christ Church was established in 1836 and is one of the oldest churches in Georgetown / IB

The Cheddi Jagan Research Centre in Georgetown celebrates the life and work of Dr Cheddi Jagan (1918-1997) who was elected Chief Minister in 1953 and Premier of British Guiana from 1957 to 1964 prior to independence. He later served as President of Guyana from 1992 to 1997. The research centre is privately run by the Jagan family and friends and was opened in 2000 / IB

St Andrew's Kirk opened its doors to the public in 1818 and for almost two hundred years its prominent steeple has graced Georgetown's skyline. It has the distinction of being the first church built by Europeans to admit enslaved Africans as worshippers / IB

St. Andrew's Kirk holds the distinction of being 'the oldest ecclesiastical building in the city'. It stands on the site believed to be the spot where the Brandwagt or signal post was erected circa 1746 or 1748. It is also believed that an Indian trading post was located somewhere on the site where the Brandwagt was erected, the former being the first sign of European civilization in the country.

The first foundation of the building intended for a Dutch Reformed Church was laid by Governor Henry William Bentinck on August 12, 1811. Services were held as early as 1812 though the structure was incomplete. By 1813, the Dutch experienced financial difficulties and the unfinished building was advertised for sale. It was sold at Execution Sale on May 4, 1813 and purchased by a few members of the Dutch Vestry.

Two years later, the Scottish community offered to meet the expenses to complete the church and to enjoy half the right and title to the building.

This was accepted by the Court of Policy and on September 27, 1818, the building was opened as St. Andrew's Church. Reverend Archibald Browne, the first Scottish Minister and the Dutch Predicant, Reverend B. Floors officiated before a crowded congregation.

St. Andrew's enjoyed a peaceful existence despite being in danger of destruction by fire in 1828. Over the years, the architecture of St. Andrew's has undergone numerous changes. The original building was smaller than present and it was planned along the lines of the Romanesque Revival Architectural Style (called Norman in England) rather than the Gothic Revival Architecture we now see.

For almost 200 years, St. Andrew's Kirk, with its high steeple and quaint double angled roof, has graced the landscape of the city. Its endearing value to the cultural landscape of the city has been identified, as it is one of the primary structures proposed for Georgetown's nomination to the UNESCO World Heritage List.

# Festivals, rituals and holidays

The vibrant, diverse culture of Guyana embodies many significant festivals, rituals and commemorations, both religious and secular; some at fixed dates of the calendar, others determined by the season.

What is interesting about celebrations in Guyana is that many of these events are not of a one-day nature - the date slated for a festival is sometimes preceded and followed by days heralding and winding down the event which are just as important as the big day itself especially if it is a religious observance.

New Year's Day is an apt point of departure, and like so many other countries, this is a national holiday. It is that lull that comes before storming into New Year; or a continuation of carousing started on Old Year's Night (Eve of New Year). However this is viewed, the Roman influence of Janus cannot be overlooked.

Next on the national calendar is Mashramani – a celebration to mark Guyana's Republic status on February 23 which is a national holiday and is regarded as one of the biggest festivities of the year. There are various activities including the Masquerade Band with its ever-increasing popularity taking to the streets. But the most spectacular activity is the float parade usually staged on Republic Day.

Also around this time, February/March, Guyana celebrates Chinese New Year with the members of the Chinese community putting on cultural shows including the exciting dragon dance and the release of sky lanterns.

Then comes Phagwah, Good Friday and Easter Monday, falling within close proximity of each other, another manifestation of our cultural diversity.

It is also useful to note that the month of April, with no known national event and which falls midway in the year, is a time to take stock especially in regards to World Book & Copyright Day.

May is awash with commemorations both religious and secular, all national holidays. May

The Rupununi Wildlife festival is a celebration of indigenous Guyanese heritage / GTA

Mashramani, often abbreviated to 'Mash', is an annual festival that celebrates Guyana becoming a Republic in 1970. The festival, usually held on 23 February (Republic Day), includes a parade, music, games and cooking and is intended to commemorate the 'Birth of the Republic' / MED

The month of December is a revered time for Christians throughout Guyana, and St George's Anglican Cathedral in the centre of Georgetown is an important venue for marking this sacred time of year / IB

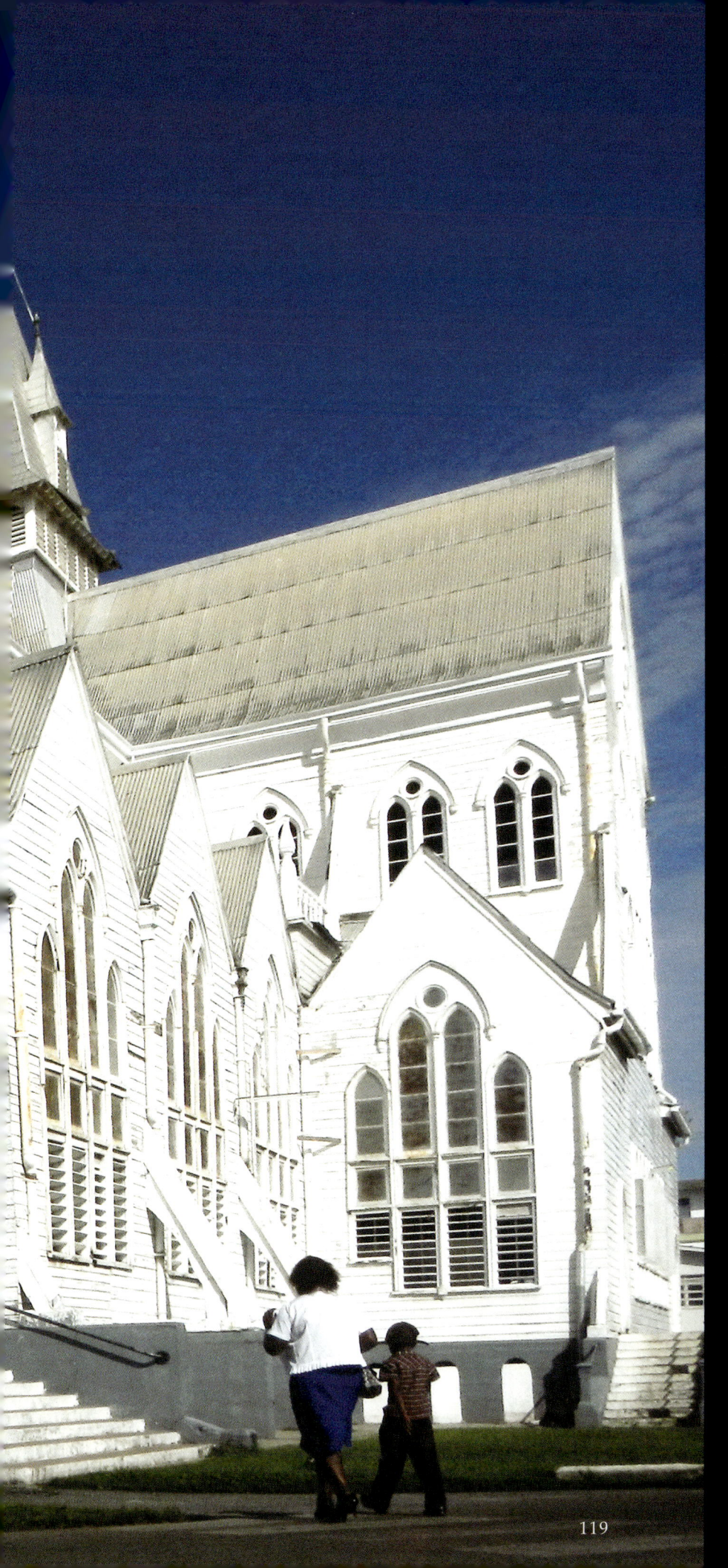

1 is Labour Day; May 5 is Arrival Day marking the arrival of our ancestors from India and honouring their descendants. May 26 is Independence Day which, in 2016, is its Golden Jubilee Year and will be celebrated with year long activities.

June 16 is Enmore Martyrs' Day commemorating the struggles in 1948 of sugar cane workers on the Enmore Estate for better working conditions that resulted in the death of five cane cutters.

On or about the 4th, the first Monday in July, falls Caricom Day celebrating the establishment of a common market among Caribbean states.

Emancipation Day is August 1 when full freedom was granted to enslaved Africans in 1834. The major activity of this National Holiday is an Emancipation Festival held in the National Park.

The month of September is dedicated to recognising the contribution of Guyana's first peoples and is labelled 'Amerindian Heritage Month'.

Eid-ul-Azha, the feast of sacrifice, falls during this month in this year.

October is the time for another spectacular show on earth. During this month the Festival of Light, Diwali, is celebrated, symbolic of the triumph of good over evil and light over darkness. The highlight of this celebration is the Diwali Motorcade, a fleet of vehicles, gaily decorated and illuminated, accompanied by children and adults in costumes, depicting various aspects of the festival, accompanied by music.

During the month of October is the Rockstone Fish Festival in the bauxite area of Linden.

December is Christmas Day, Boxing Day both National Holidays.

Youman Nabi, the birth anniversary of Prophet Muhammad, falls during this month of the year.

End of December, Old Year's Night (New Year's Eve) is a very busy time for church-goers and party animals. One of the traditions of the night is to eat cook-up rice at the dawning of the New Year in order to ensure prosperity in the coming year.

The Georgetown Seawall is not just a barrier to hold back the tide but an important space on which many celebrants perform their rituals. During the year you can witness kite flying; the planting of jhandi flags on the seashore – another spectacle of flowing colours against the

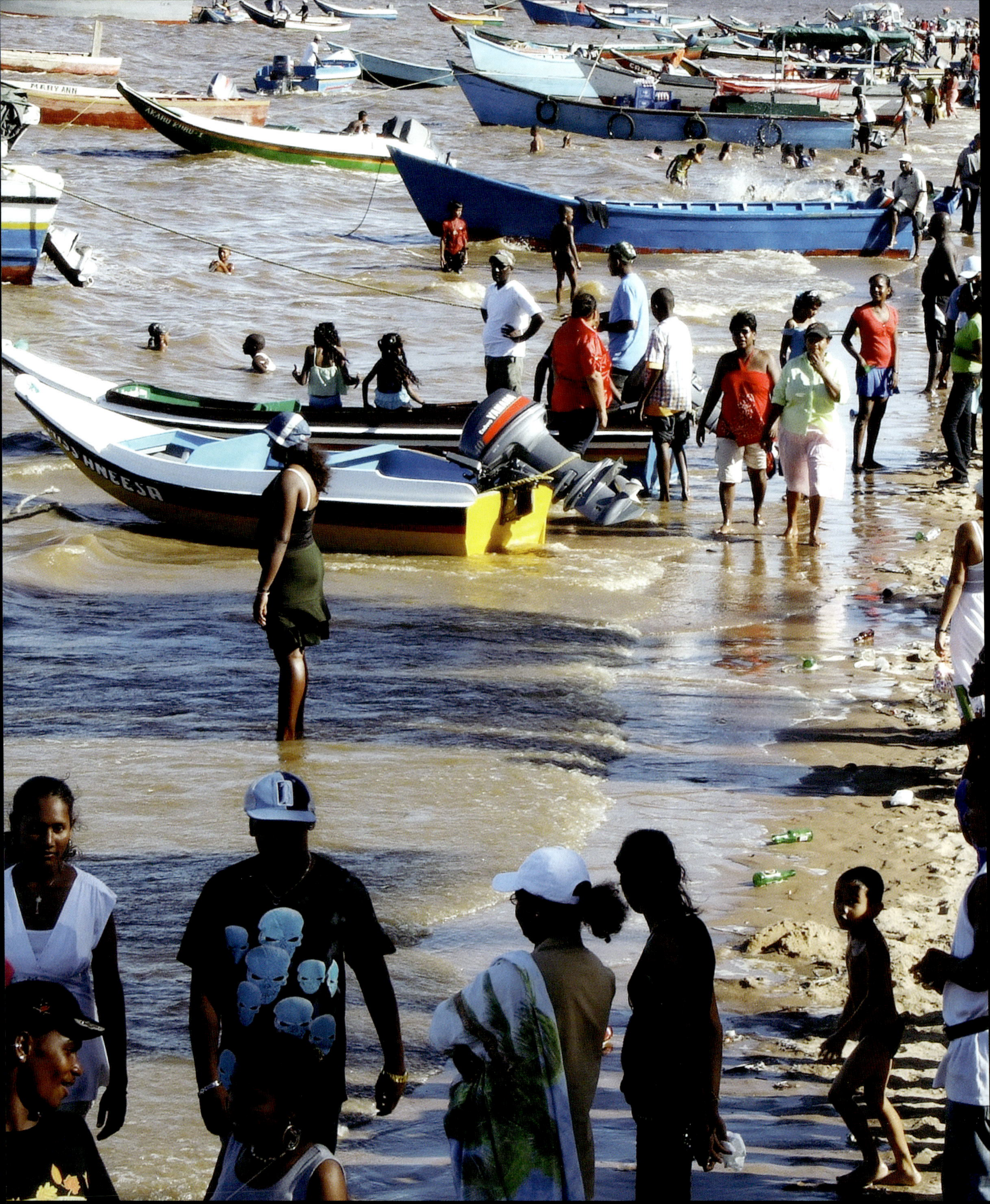

An enthusiastic young drummer celebrating Phagwah / IB

mud flats and muddy waters; Holocaust Day when the descendants of enslaved Africans pay homage to their ancestors; Kali Mai Puja, Kartik Nahan/Snaan festival when Hindus offer prayers to their Gods and Goddesses, taking baths in the salt water, symbolic of washing away bad karma and returning to a state of purity and prosperity.

And we are not finished. In the open-air celebratory atmosphere of Guyana, there are many instances of rituals, celebrations and festivities that are not confined to a day in the calendar. The best example of this is the maticore and kwe-kwe, both wedding initiation rituals. They take place anytime of the year, usually before a wedding, acquainting or reminding the bride of her 'wifely responsibilities'.

Visitors to Guyana are spoilt for choice, as anytime of the year you will be able to see and participate in a festival or celebration.

Emancipation Day marks the abolition of slavery on 1st August 1834. Tiger Island (aka Hamburg Island) is a popular venue for marking this important occasion / GTA

*Petamber Persaud*

Children's Costume and Float Parade celebrating Guyana's 50th anniversary of Independence / MED

The Hindu festival of Phagwah celebrates the triumph of good over evil. Participants usually wear white or light-coloured clothing and douse each other with coloured powder or a red liquid known as abeer / IB

Musicians and revellers gather for 'Mash' celebrations / MED

# "... If but a wind blows, all her beauty wakes[1] ..."

A.J. Seymour's *Name Poem* (1946) evokes Guyana as a beautiful cosmopolitan place. It is a kaleidoscope of histories, places, stories, images, memories, ideas, sounds, tastes, inventions, retentions and suppositions about similarities and difference embedded in and influenced by particular relationships of people to *space*.

The country is lush in every sense of this word. Nestled between the rising bosom of Roraima and the meandering manhood of the Atlantic Ocean, today's Guyanese have retained customs and practices that form the basis of an emerging Guyanese Creole culture. This incorporates linguistic, culinary, performance, religious, business, intellectual, scientific, visual and artistic traditions. The milieu has been consciously co-created and negotiated since Guyana began its struggle for self-governance from the British and thereafter since independence in 1966.

Fifty years of multi-ethnic co-inhabitation and adaptable use of local flora and fauna has produced a diversely sumptuous national cuisine. This includes pepperpot, a wide range of cassava based dishes and wild meats from the first nations; rice based dishes such as cook-up, fried rice, shine-rice and sweet-rice.

Locally grown organic ground provisions are central to local cooking including dishes like metem-gee, boil and fry, cassava pone, quinches and sweet potato salads and chips. A wide range of vegetable and provision soups, dhals, curries and pasta dishes like chow meins and special Guyanese style macaroni and cheese along with many flour based dishes like rotis, puris, tennis rolls, Chinese cakes, breads and desserts like black cake, conkee, pone and mithai make up a distinct Guyanese menu. Several African and Indian food staples have now become national delicacies. These include, garlic pork, chicken foot and trotters souse, black pudding, mauby, bush teas and sugar cake. These gastronomic delights are washed

1. Line from A.J. Seymour's 'Name Poem' (1946)

Abundant vegetation, lush rainforests teeming with spectacular wildlife and a rich and vibrant culture are what make Guyana so enticing / DH-GTA

Many of the country's indigenous music and dances, though now secular in appearance, have ethnic, ritual or religious bases. Constitutionally committed to religious tolerance, Guyana is home to several religions including Christianity, Islam, Hinduism, Buddhism, Khali, Rastafarianism, Bahi, Hari Krishna, and Jordanites. The richness and range of religious musics that accompany these are amazing. There is Masquerade retained from African yam festivals. There are hymns and Christian pop music, bhajans, chowtals, tazias and a range of African, Muslim and Hindu language religious musics.

Unique to Guyana are the ethnic traditions that have infused wedding rituals in Guyana - Kwe-kwe and Matticore, African and Indian pre-nuptials are incorporated into both Christian as well as Hindu weddings.

Apart from religious festivals and Guyana's carnival, Mashramani, exciting new festivals include the Rupunini Culture and Arts Festival, Iwokrama Environment and Archery Festival, Guyfesta Arts Festival and G-Jazz Music Festival.

Though Guyanese popular music and dance has been highly influenced in the last 50 years by American rhythm and blues, Trinidadian soca and Jamaican dancehall, four important indigenous musical developments are notable. The development of the Shanto (precursor to soca music), chutney (pioneered in the 1970s by Guyanese), calistro (fusion of First peoples Mari-Mari with Afro Brazilian beats) and a vibrant and innovative cottage recording and broadcasting industry which have kept Guyanese sound alive.

Other Guyanese sound traditions include bird whistling races, military band and live pop band music including steelpan, rock and rhythm and blues. Genres are comprehensive and diverse ranging from Indian classical and folk music to African pop, choral, country and western, classical, jazz, instrumental, reggae, to dancehall and chutney.

Traditional dances of various ethnic groups are still publicly performed as part of the national repertoire. This repertoire is distinctly diverse and multi-cultural with evidence of Cuban style ballet, African Ijbo, Masquerade, Indian Kathack or Bhojpuri folk dances, First Nations Mari-Mari's, Chinese dragon dances, tassa and conga drum based African and Indian dance steps in modern dance pieces. There is also a growing Latin dance tradition heavily influenced by the large numbers of Brazilians, Cubans and Venezuelans settled in Guyana in the last 25 years.

It is therefore not uncommon for all types of music to be played in one night at a party with all Guyanese present naturally and automatically switching their dance movements in accordance with the type of music being played. Such is the fluidity and dynamism of the Guyanese cultural complex.

Performativity and reflexivity have been historically central to cultural production in Guyana. Historical ethnic, oral and euro-centric literary traditions have within the last 50 years co-created an incredible and celebrated national intellectual, literary and performance output. Since independence Guyana has produced hundreds of national and internationally respected scholars and educators in various fields and as many prize winning playwrights, novelists, poets and performers in all genres ranging from music to stage and film.

Themes of identity, social history, ethnicity, politics, environment, conflict, love and metaphysics dominate national literary productions. Recently, Guyanese biography has emerged with 88 historical volumes reprinted under the nationally owned Caribbean Press. Otherwise several compelling stories of modern Guyanese, some of whom are still alive, have appeared; many introduced through Guyana's prestigious Prize for Literature.

Inextricably linked to the nascent national aesthetic has been language. A peculiarly Guyanese set of English Creoles based on African, Portuguese and Indian dialects has emerged both in spoken word and written text. To the trained ear, distinct other languages are spoken and understood by the vast majority of Guyanese.

The visual art production is as stunning as the country's magnificent flora and fauna and the gorgeous people immortalised in artefact. Long traditions in sculpting, acrylic painting and pottery have produced well developed and dominant forms and artists.

Photography, videography, textiles and cinema are emerging rapidly. Within the last fifty years, euro-centric oeuvre, sensibilities and techniques have gradually given way to a Mezzo-American Guyanese aesthetic centred around local themes and scenes, local materials and techniques as well as personalising of styles sometimes based on ethno-cultural consciousness.

Celebrated on Republic Day, Mashramani includes a vivacious street parade and music to commemorate the 'Birth of the Republic' / MED

A celebration of Amerindian heritage / KJ

Phagwah (Holi) Day celebrations / IB

Lokono art is a distinctive feature as well as marvellously complex wood carvings from variegated local woods. Spires, minarets and totem poles complement each other architecturally in Guyana, especially in the capital Georgetown in which grand colonial buildings and modernist architecture meet.

There is also a great jewellery making tradition featuring distinct ethno-centric designs in silver, gold, precious and semi-precious stones found in Guyana as well as seeds and plant particles.

Though fashion in Guyana overwhelmingly reflects the country's nexus to North America, within the last fifteen years a native fashion sense has been developed based on readings of climate, cultural sensitivity and national distinctiveness.

Guyana is cricket country. However, there are strong racing, shooting, track and field, boxing, football, racquet game, golfing, swimming, bird whistling and fishing traditions which have been maintained over the years. Board games like dominoes, cards, bridge and chess are also national favourites.

Guyana is a gently exciting cosmopolitan space in which there is something and somewhere for everyone. The openness this produces has preserved Guyana's reputation as the most lovely and hospitable country in the Caribbean over these fifty years of its independence.

*Dr Paloma Mohamed Martin is the Anthony N. Sabga Caribbean Award for Excellence, Arts & Letters Laureate 2015*

A feast of local delights / KJ

## PORTRAIT FOR ME
by Paloma Mohamed Martin

Paint me a blue parrot,
white frangipani, coral moon in dark purple sky.
Paint me Makonaima[1]'s green bearded mountains,
bronzed Buxton spice and yellow plantain,
weaves of rice or Eti palms, annatto hieroglyphs of sun Gods.
Paint me cocoa lovers locked on grey sea walls,
dark phallic statues of slaves rising,
Essequibo's red bosom heaving,
Buffianda[2] and Dougla[3] girls,
Bora[4] bracelets on earth-brown hands,
Santantone[5] seamen with Snapper
and Trout coming in to land.
Paint canoes, red-black water,
emerald mansions of trees,
Burrowes'[6] bowl of fruit, Mittleholzer[7]'s magic flute.
Paint cock-of- the-rock, tiny golden frog[8],
twenty falls tumbling froth.
Paint me bridges that float and citified goats.
Paint me fires that burn, brown waters that rise,
paint silver hope in their eyes.
Paint mouths open chanting,
arrows gold gleaming, unfettered feet dancing,
    child's pink-heart beating....

Paint me this portrait love, of my native land.

1. Makonaima – great spirit of the first peoples said to dwell in the highest of high places where the land meets the clouds
2. Mixture of First Peoples and African
3. Mixture of East Indian and African
4. Bora is a nutritious string bean grown bountifully in the country and beloved by most Guyanese
5. Portuguese and African, Asian or First Peoples mixture
6. E.R. Burrowes – famous Guyanese painter
7. Edgar Mittlelholzer – the Caribbean's first published novelist was from Guyana. One of his novels was *My Bones and My Flute* and features a flute that played otherworldly music
8. Rare frog which inhabits area around the majestic Kaieteur Falls in Guyana

Hindu prayer flags (jhandi) / IB

Mashramani ('Mash') celebrations / MED

## A diverse musical heritage

From our very earliest cultural experiences in Guyana, there have been musical expressions that have shaped and defined the nation. The indigenous peoples developed musical patterns and crafted musical instruments out of the materials they found around them and used music as an integral element of their cultural and religious practices. And with the coming of the other ethnic groups the country's musical fabric was expanded and developed. The outcome is a rich and varied tapestry that is not just an expression of the variety of cultural styles that are extant in the society but an amalgamation, a potpourri, shaping its reality as much as it is being shaped by it.

Colonialism played an important role in the country's musical development, bringing with it both the militaristic and the mundane. The imperative of stratification for societal control ensured that music was used both as control mechanism and for segregation. The upper classes took their cues from Europe, as did those with societal ambition, propagating and idealising classical styles, while those from the lower classes forged out of their psyches the music of disenfranchisement, wrought in suffering and yet abundant with passion and panache.

Contact with neighbouring Caribbean nations would also contribute to the discourse and out of this would emerge music that would define the country, becoming the fertile ground in which regional idioms would emerge.

British Guiana was the centre of musical development as early as the 1930s, with some of the significant Caribbean players making this country their Mecca. In 1934, Bill Rogers (Augustus Hinds) sailed by ship to the United States and recorded, for the RCA Blue Bird, the biggest record label at the time, thirty-four of his songs. This was done in Camden, New Jersey and by 1937, Bill Rogers was in Trinidad, where he impressively won the calypso crown for that year. He was the first Guyanese to do so.

The Mighty Sparrow, among others, would come to Guyana to 'learn the ropes' and along with these musicians came the steelpan, which would transform the musical landscape and forge a Caribbean collective that still exerts tremendous influence on the musical styles being practiced today.

Calypso, soca, chutney, reggae; these are the styles of music that are considered 'Guyanese' today and while their roots seem to have been in other countries in the region, the free flow of ideas and movement conspired to give them credence across the broad panoply that is defined as 'Caribbean'. Common experiences and connection transcended the boundaries of space and left a legacy that, like the sport of cricket, speaks to intrinsic integration. That it is music without its baggage of language, that shows how connected the countries of the region are is instructive.

Bill Rogers (real name Augustus Hinds) at a recording session in 1972 in Georgetown / RH

Lester 'De Professor' Charles was crowned Calypso Monarch in 2016 for the fifth time in his career / MED

Terry Gajraj is Guyana's soca and chutney superstar. Internationally renowned, he has performed throughout the Caribbean and in North America, the United Kingdom, mainland Europe and India / KJ

Clockwise from top: Panorama champions 2016, Panwave Parkside steelband; nineteen-year-old Junior Calypso Monarch 2016, T'Shanna Cort; calypso veteran, Lady Tempest (Camille Goliah) / MED

Guyana is once again coming into its own, musically. The thrust towards self-sufficiency is strong on the agenda; the collective artistic and creative psyche is once again stretching towards a uniquely 'Guyanese' expression. But none of this would be possible without the creation of an industry that moves from the creation of music to its distribution and sale.

The government is committed to the introduction of modern copyright legislation that will bring Guyana into the mainstream internationally, and reward artists for their intellectual contribution and artistry. Cultural industries have contributed significantly to the development of other Caribbean countries and Guyana is working to ensure that music not only becomes a garner of foreign exchange but a driver of tourism.

The Ministry of Education sees music as integral to a child's holistic development and the reintroduction of the singing of National Songs into the school curriculum, together with a commitment to establish steel bands in schools across the country, are key elements of the programme to harness musical talent and encouraged appreciation and participation.

There is a renewed energy and commitment to the propagation of a local music industry and it is hoped that this will be a lasting legacy that will see Guyana take its place as a significant player in the regional musical establishment. Music defines a country's image and Guyana is now on the threshold of forging a unique Guyanese brand to share with the world.

*Russel Lancaster*

Small bananas known locally as 'Parika figs' / KJ

Fruit and vegetable stands are a common sight throughout Guyana / IB

A wide variety of fish including baskets of the popular hassar / IB

# Cooking Guyanese style

Over the past fifty years, Guyanese have carved out a unique blend of mouth-watering dishes unique and distinctive to them.

They love their foods hot, both temperature-wise and pepper-wise. Temperature-wise, who doesn't love a hot dhal or a hot pepperpot; pepper-wise, the choice is endless, with black pepper even in desserts (pones).

A cold glass of coconut water, cane juice, mauby or swank (lime drink) and most definitely a cold cup of ice cream with jello can accompany any meal.

Here are some of the favourite recipes of traditional Guyanese foods.

## Curried Duck
Ingredients: 4 lbs duck, 2 oz curry powder, ¼ tsp black pepper, 2 tbsps chopped fine thyme, 1 tbsp chopped broad leaf thyme, 1 tbsp ground geera, 1 tbsp garam massala, 1 tsp brown sugar, 1 tsp ground spice, 2 medium onions, chopped, 2 cloves garlic, crushed, 4 medium potatoes, peeled and cut in quarters, Salt to taste

Method: Wash prepared duck and cut into neat pieces. Season duck with salt, black pepper, thyme and crushed garlic. Mix curry powder, geera and garam masala with a little water to form a paste. Fry curry paste and onion in a little oil, add meat and fry. Add meat stock, bring to the boil and cook on a slow fire until meat is tender. Add sugar, spice and potatoes. Simmer lightly until potatoes are fully cooked. Serve hot with Demerara Rice, Roti or Dhal Puri.

## Metemgee (Metagee)
Ingredients: 1 dry coconut, ¾ lb mixed meat (optional), 1 lb salted fish, 1 lb cassava, 1 lb plantain (your choice of ripeness), 1 lb eddoes, or dasheen, 1 lb yams, 1 large onion, cut in rings, ½ lb ochroes (okra). Dumplings: ½ cup cornmeal, ½ cup flour, 1 tbsp baking powder, 2 tbsps margarine, ¼ tsp salt, 1 tbsp sugar

Method: Grate coconut and infuse with 1 pt. hot water. Cover the mixed meat with water and boil for ½ hour. Put salt-fish to soak in water, then strain off that water and boil in fresh water until tender. Flake or process boiled salt fish. Squeeze the coconut mixture and strain to extract the coconut milk. Pour over the meat. Peel the vegetables, and then add to the coconut milk. Cook until almost tender. Mix all ingredients for dumplings together and add enough water to form stiff dough. Shape into eight balls. Add about 10 minutes before the vegetables are ready. Cover the pot tightly. Remove dumplings after this time and place in a serving platter. Fry salted fish with onions and place on serving platter.

## Pepperpot
Ingredients: 1 lb cow heel, 2 lbs brisket, 2 lbs oxtail, ½ lb tripe, ½ pt casareep, 2 wiri wiri peppers, 2 one inch dried cinnamon sticks, 1-2 inch piece dried orange peel, 1 star anise, 3 cloves, 2 oz sugar, Salt to taste

Method: Wipe and clean meat thoroughly. Put heels to boil or cook in a pressure cooker for about 15 minutes. Add the other meats to the cooked cow heel. Cook by simmering gently for about one hour. Add casareep and other ingredients. Adjust flavour with salt and sugar. This dish develops flavour when left over a period of days. It must be reheated to boiling point daily.

Paratha roti / KJ

Chow Mein / KJ

## Chicken Chow Mein

Ingredients: 2 pkts chow mein noodles, 1 chicken, cut in pieces, ½ cup mixed seasoning, 1 bundle bora, 2 medium carrots, cut in strips, 2 red bell peppers, cut in cubes, 2 large onions, chopped, 2 tbsps soy sauce, 1 tbsp Chinese spice, oil for frying, black pepper, 2 tbsps chopped celery, 2 tbsps chopped shallot, salt to taste

Method: Wash chicken and season with your favourite seasoning mix. Bring 4 pints of water to the boil in a large pot. Add 1 tbsp. of salt to the boiling water. Break up chow mein noodles into smaller pieces and place in boiling water. Boil until tender enough for a fork to cut through, but not soft. Strain immediately in a colander and rinse under cold running water. Put the oil in a large frying pan and heat. Add chicken and stir and fry until cooked. Add hot water along the way, so that chicken cooks thoroughly. Set aside. Wash and prepare frying pan to stir-fry the carrots, bora, onions and bell peppers. Add a little oil and fry vegetables. Add chicken and chow mein and continue stirring, while frying. Add soy sauce, Chinese spice, celery and shallots. Toss in sweet corn. Adjust flavour with salt. Garnish with tomatoes and parsley and serve hot

## Shepherd's Pie

Ingredients: 1 lb lean minced beef, 1 tbsp oil, ¼ cup mixed chopped herbs (shallots, celery, onions), 1 tbsp flour, 2 lbs potatoes, ¼ cup milk, 2 tbsps tomato sauce, 1 onion, chopped, 1 tbsp soy sauce, salt to taste. To garnish: 1 small sprig parsley, 1 cup grated cheese

Method: Wash and peel potatoes and put to boil. Crush while hot with the milk. Place the oil in a frying pan. Add the mince and seasonings and fry. Add the soy sauce, tomato ketchup and flour to thicken. Grease a medium sized oven dish, add half of the crushed potato to the bottom. Spread evenly over dish. Add minced beef and arrange evenly over the potatoes. Cover with the remainder of potatoes. Mark out with a fork and then spread the grated cheese on top. Bake in a hot oven until browned at the top or brown under a broiler. Garnish with a sprig of parsley and a strip of sweet pepper and serve.

## Garlic Pork

Ingredients: 3-4 lbs lean pork or spare ribs, 2 pts vinegar, ½ lb garlic, peeled and crushed, 1 bunch fine thyme, 2 broad leaf thyme, 6 wiri wiri peppers, 4-6 cloves, salt to taste.

Method: Cut into suitable sized pieces. Wash pork in a solution of ¼ pint vinegar and 1 pint water. Place in a large jar or bottle. Pound peppers and thyme. Add pepper garlic, salt and clove to the remainder of vinegar. Pour over pork ensuring that it completely covered with the liquid. Leave to soak for about 3 to 4 days. When ready to cook the pork, heat a frying pan slightly. Add the pork together with some of the liquid in which it was soaked. Leave it to boil until some of the liquid evaporates. The fat from the pork will then begin to melt and be enough to fry the pork until it is brown. Serve with home-made bread or rolls.

Mauby / KJ

First consumed by the indigenous peoples of Guyana, cassava bread is still made in the traditional way. Today, the biscuit-like staple is eaten by all Guyanese and is generally consumed with pepperpot or any other meat or fish dish / KJ

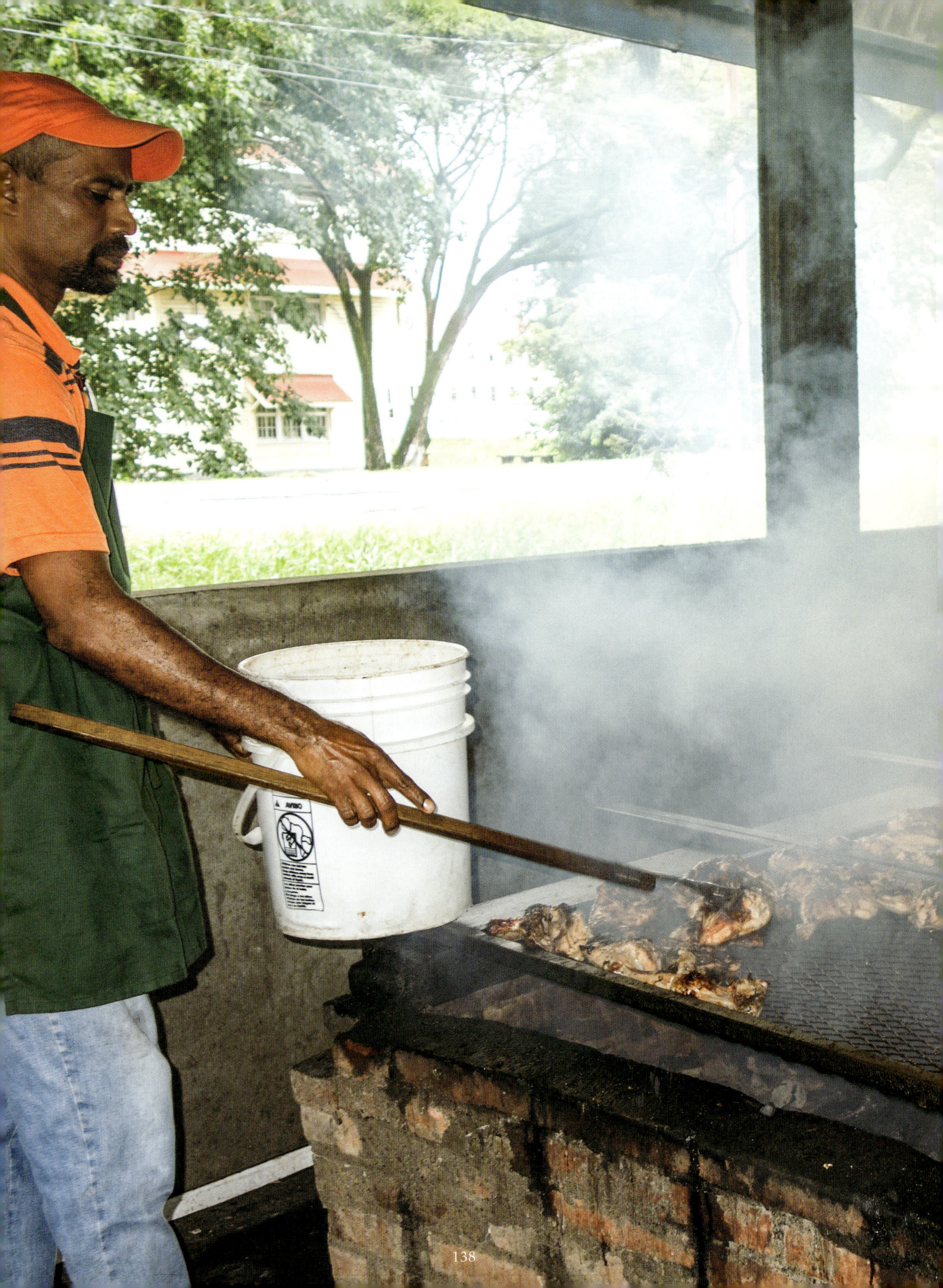

Barbecue chicken on an industrial scale / IB

# Sport & Pastimes

Culturally, Guyana is Caribbean, and cricket is part of the fabric of Caribbean culture / IB

Providence Stadium, or the Guyana National Stadium, replaced Bourda as the national stadium and was built specifically to host Super Eight matches in the 2007 Cricket World Cup / IB

Kennard Memorial Turf Club races at its Bush Lot Farm racecourse in Corentyne / DH-GTA

Sport & Pastimes

Road cycling is a popular sport which is governed by the Guyana Cycling Federation / IB

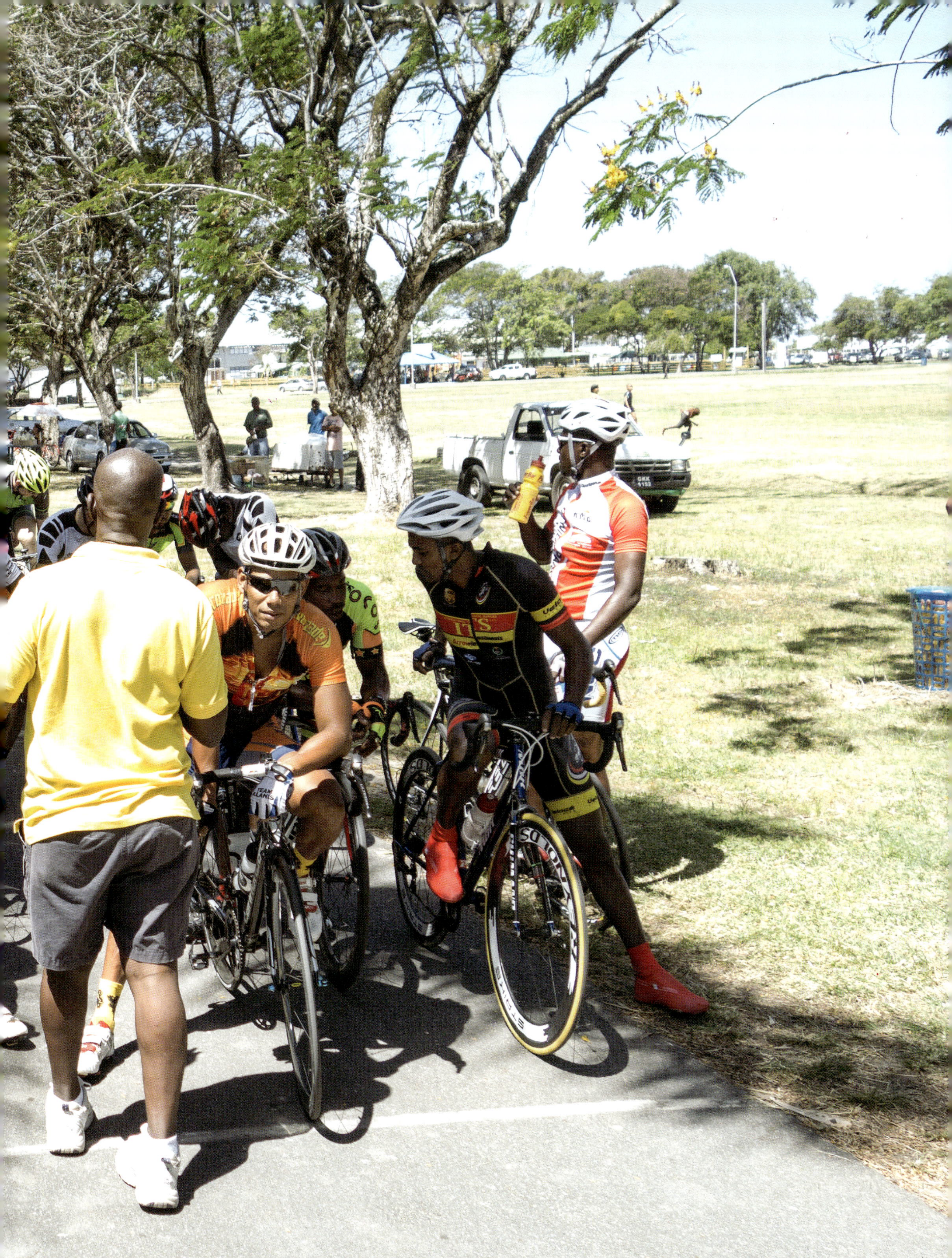

# Sport & Pastimes

Guyana has produced six professional world championship boxers and, in 1980, an Olympic bronze medallist / KJ

Club swimmers training at the National Aquatic Centre in Georgetown / IB

The annual Rupununi Rodeo in Lethem takes place over the Easter weekend / DH-GTA

A game of draughts at Parika ferry stelling / IB

Sport & Pastimes

The hinterland football pitches, such as this one in Rupununi, have nurtured a rich source of footballing talent / IB

The essence of true Demerara sugar is in the sugar cane from Guyana / JB

## Distinctively Guyanese or uniquely Guyanese

Guyana can lay claim to many unique features or distinctive characteristics, notably its flora and fauna that stand above those of any other country in the world. But little know are these three features that are uniquely and distinctively Guyanese.

## DEMERARA SUGAR

**If it's not from Demerara, it's not 'Demerara'**

In 1832, at the Vreed-en-Hoop sugar estate on the west bank of the Demerara River, an innovative process involving the use of a vacuum pan with steam energy was introduced in the manufacturing of sugar. The crystals produced were so refined and of such superior quality that they could no longer be categorised as 'muscovado' sugar – the dark, sticky sugar commonly produced in the British colonies at the time.

This product was re-classified by the British authorities as 'Demerara crystals' and subsequently referred to as "Demerara sugar".

Since then, there have been many incarnations of Demerara sugar, with the name, 'Demerara' being adopted by sugar producing countries throughout the world. Even beet sugar manufacturers are producing 'Demerara' sugar, and the term has become generic for just about any type of brown sugar.

Indeed, much of the 'Demerara' sugar sold internationally is actually refined sugar coated with molasses.

Legal recognition of the term 'Demerara sugar' as a sugar produced in the Demerara region of British Guiana was ended in November 1913 by a decision of the High Court of Justice in London. A magistrate dismissed the case against the sale of sugar described as 'Demerara sugar' (but not the genuine article) on the grounds that the expression had become a "conventional term for the yellow crystal sugar not necessarily produced in Demerara".

The Oxford English Dictionary defines – origin: from the region of *Demerara* in Guyana. Ninety years after the court ruling the Guyana Sugar Corporation (GuySuCo), the only producer of genuine Demerara cane sugars, took steps to revalidate the dictionary's definition of the term 'Demerara sugar' and regain global recognition of the product's original source.

In 2003, the corporation launched its first branded, pre-packaged sugar, 'Demerara Gold', a natural brown sugar made from the finest quality canes. Since then, Demerara Gold has established itself as the premium sugar in Guyana and many Caribbean countries as well as obtaining new and burgeoning markets in the US and UK. The corporation hopes that in time, and under the new dispensations for global trade and intellectual property recognition, the world will come to recognise that if it does not come from Demerara, it is not 'Demerara'.

## THE TAPIR

There is more to the tapir than meets the eye. Not the animal but the vehicle unique to that name. And unique to Guyana.

In 1974, while Guyana was experiencing its worst economic crisis due mainly to rising fuel prices, Ainlim, a local company, started the assembling of a light-weight vehicle that was to consume less gas and travel many more miles per gallon of fuel. It could take up to seven passengers. This brought some relief to embattled drivers. But things changed with the advent of the mini-bus – a faster and more suitable passenger vehicle catering for more passengers.

So the production of the tapir vehicle ceased sometime in the early 1980s. Obviously the remaining tapirs that were serviceable were forced to adapt to the competition. These are now plying their trade in Berbice, traversing short distances mainly between Crabwood Creek and # 64 & # 55 Villages on the upper

The distinct and unique tapirs / IB

One major difference between the animal, known as the 'bush cow' in Guyana, and this box-like vehicle is colour. While the animal sports a drab outfit, the vehicle is dabbed in hues of butterflies and flowers and rainbows. It's a thrill to see colours rushing up to you and rushing past. The colour is like a code and identity; regular users can identify a vehicle by its colours.

The decorated tapir can carry as many as ten nametags – from 'Juvenile' to 'Never Trust a Stranger' - that identify the vehicle, like its decorative motifs, and set it apart from its competitors. Such unique and distinctive brandings are a virtual badge of honour for each vehicle. These names also have resonances to the lingua franca of the city like 'Flight Cracks', 'Brush', 'Silent Future' and 'After Effect'. Names that also have hidden but understood meanings. Many use the word 'original' with another like 'move'; so you will see 'original move', and 'original this and original that'; a method used by many drivers/owners staking a claim to pioneering the tapir as a distinctive and unique product of the country. *Petamber Persaud*

## GUYANA MAGENTA STAMP

The British Guiana One-Cent Magenta stamp is now the most valuable stamp in the history of the world, reputed to be worth over US $9 million. It was printed in Georgetown and first issued on 4 April 1856.

This stamp has an interesting history from its one-cent value to its current price and its journey from Guyana to the United States.

Running low on postage stamps, the then Post Master in British Guiana, Mr E.T.E. Dalton, commissioned local printers and publishers of the Official Gazette, Joseph Baum and William Dallas, to produce an emergency issue of one-cent and four-cent stamps.

Not many of the one-cent stamps were printed but one turned up in 1873. Louis Vernon Vaughn, a 12-year-old, found one among his uncle's letters and sold it for six shillings to a wealthy local stamp collector, N.R. McKennon.

Five years later, in 1878, McKennon's collection was sold to an English philatelist, Thomas Ridpath of Liverpool, England, for £120. He in turn, later sold the stamp to Phillipp von Ferrary for £150.

Ferrary's stamp collection was originally willed to a Berlin museum in Germany but on his death in 1917, the entire collection was taken to France as war reparations at the end of the First World War.

In 1922, American industrialist Arthur Hind bought the stamp for US $32,500, making it, for the first time, the most valuable stamp in the world. Having changed hands and been the subject of litigation, the British Guiana One-Cent Magenta stamp was sold on 17 June 2014 at an auction for US $9,480,00. The new owner, Stuart Weitzman, broke the world record for a single stamp with his purchase.

The stamp is now on display until 2017 at the Smithsonian's National Postal Museum in Washington, DC.

# *What's trending in Guyana?*

In the last ten years alone, Guyana has seen a gradual change in the things that fuel the entertainment, passions and even social interactions of her people. This is due largely in part to the emergence and proliferation of social media.

Now, with the newfound power given to the common people via social media platforms, Guyanese have received a boost in confidence and have joined the world of people who had already begun to utilise this medium to have their voices heard. In a society where people were for years frustrated and silenced by political and other powers, many quickly gravitated to social media. As internet access increased across the country, platforms such as Facebook grew in popularity among Guyanese, and soon, it became the main outlet for expression and democracy.

The influence of social media was greatly seen during the 2015 General Elections. After 23 years of rule by one administration, the people had been exhausted by the inability to be heard. With everyone now having the power to speak at their fingertips, many took to publicly voicing their opinions which in turn fostered national conversation. It was the first type of 'trending' that occurred in Guyana, where political figures were immediately placed under the microscope of public scrutiny, making them answerable for their deeds. At last, the public had the power, and among them included a large number of young people, who prior to the modern age of technology had little to no outlet that they could relate to. The sort of transparency that was provided by social media, therefore, made it hard for things to be done in the dark.

Seeing how social media carved the narrative of an event as major as the General Elections, it became clear to Guyanese that their newfound voice was not to be silenced. With their renewed sense of confidence, what we find today is a bolder population of people with a strengthened sense of identity and patriotism. Some people developed such a strong voice that they picked up a large following, as people clamoured to their Facebook and other accounts to see what these people had to say. The growth in online news and citizen reporters also increased, with many opting to leave behind traditional means of getting news to using the internet to access and share it.

Granted, the power of social media is nothing new. The world has been utilising platforms like YouTube, Facebook and Twitter for years. But Guyana had for quite some time been behind in these developments due to limited access to internet and technological devices. However, with

*Social media has provided a new voice for Guyanese / KJ*

the discontinuing of dial-up internet in 2012 and the subsequent introduction of high speed DSL broadband internet in wider parts of the country within the decade, Guyanese have quickly caught up on all the years they had missed. Moreover, affordable smart phones, tablets and other technological devices began to flood the markets, giving the average Guyanese the power to speak in the palm of their hands.

But it isn't just politics alone that has been affected. Thanks to social media, the local arts industry has also begun to flourish, with young people using these platforms to teach themselves skills and promote their self-taught skills to the world. It has also allowed Guyanese the opportunity of participation in the support of their people who represent the country on the international stage. Now, Facebook and other user-friendly sites are used to encourage voter participation in competitions such as global pageants and other events. It is therefore endearing to see thousands of Guyanese involved in enthusiastic efforts to support local ambassadors in these events all in the name of using their voice and their newfound power to make a mark on a wider scale.

All in all, the transformation in the confidence, thought processes and social interactions of Guyanese seen within the last decade alone is nothing less than inspiring. And as the world continues to develop, it is refreshing to know that Guyana is now and will continue to be part of that global conversation, thanks to the opportunities provided by the interconnectivity of social media.

*Jasmaine Payne is a freelance writer for the* Guyana Chronicle *newspaper*

## World recognition for Guyana's arts industry

The arts industry in Guyana is the epitome of what one would refer to as a hidden gem. For years, artists have thrived mostly on love and passion for their work, seeing little to no remuneration or recognition for their talents. In recent times, however, while this is still the case, the emergence of social media platforms like Youtube, Instagram and Facebook has made it such that the world is within their reach. A new generation of artists has begun to tap into these possibilities, teaching themselves through material on the web and promoting themselves on the same platforms while bringing evolution to the arts industry.

### MUSIC

Perhaps the first beacon of hope for the local music industry was the Guyana Telephone & Telegraph (GT&T) Cellink Plus Jingle and Song Competition in 2005. Using its first winner, a then 17-year-old Timeka Marshall, as an example, the promoters pushed the young songstress to her highest heights, making her become the country's first 'modern day Guyanese celebrity'.

At a time when the Barbadian beauty with Guyanese heritage, Rihanna, had catapulted to international stardom, much effort was plugged into the aesthetically pleasing Timeka in attempts to imitate that fame. Years later, Timeka is now living in Jamaica and has since released a number of local singles, along with some memorable collaborations with regional stars.

Meanwhile, the Jingle and Song competition – which over the years has evolved to include a television production and even a Bollywood segment - remains a catalyst through which many young artistes made their voices heard. What it did, was bring talent home.

Moreover, what Guyanese realised was that there was more than just mediocre talent on our shores. In fact, many of our 'powerhouses' who now enjoy relative local fame have gotten their start from this competition: Jackie Hanover, the reggae and soca queen; Poonam Singh, Miss Global International 2016 and social media local celebrity; and of course Lisa Punch who Guyanese have come to accept as our biggest celebrity to date.

Apart from giving Guyanese a reason to cheer when she competed in the ABC television show 'Rising Star', Lisa went on to make the country proud on the Miss World Stage in Sanya, China by winning the Talent Segment – a first for Guyana in all of this competition's history.

### PHOTOGRAPHY

Gone are the days when taking a professional photograph occurred solely on occasion; where a photo studio with tacky props and cartoon backgrounds would serve as the only source for an important occasion. Today, a bevy of young men and women have taken to the streets to capture moments in time and to share these moments with a seemingly hungry public. The public in turn, with easy access to these artists, now also take full advantage of utilising these talents to produce their own personal collection of shots to be used at will. It is the perfect example of merging art with everyday life; photography has morphed from being just a hobby, or a means of earning income, to being a bit of both and then some.

Here in Guyana, there are names that are usually tossed around as to who does what in the field of photography. In the area of nude photography, many may have heard of Brian

Gomes; others may easily identify the work of young Saajid Husani for his clean and provocative fashion photography; while others may think of Azikiwe Denheart for his well-known portraits and wedding shots. Yet, the truth is that many photographers all dabble in varying aspects of this wide ranging art, and the quality and passion with which they practice this art produce a result worthy of recognition.

## FASHION

Even before the emerging popularity of other forms of art, fashion for a long time held the public's attention with designers like Michelle Cole and Sonia Noel being household names.

Over the years, the fashion industry has evolved to include a vibrant array of young designers along with the models who saunter gracefully on and off the runway. It is these household names who in turn went on to birth another generation for the industry. Guyana is now very much known for its Guyana Fashion Week during which renowned regional and local designers show their work. More so, Sonia Noel's Guyana Model Search and Designer's Portfolio have created opportunities for designers and models alike. What is more, models have now gained legitimate representation through the likes of Traits Model Management, which in turn provides locals the thrust to walk on international stages like New York Fashion Week.

Sonia Noel

## WRITING, ART AND OTHER INDUSTRIES

Of course, other industries have seen significant growth, with youth tapping into previously ignored talents and placing themselves out in the open for the world to see. Makeup artistry is one such talent that has seen significant growth, with young women gravitating towards the art and showcasing their talents via social media.

Writing has also developed quite a following, but in a more expressive way, with the majority of 'writers' gravitating towards spoken word poetry. The spoken word movement is relatively active in Guyana, having enjoyed ten years at the recently closed Upscale Restaurant.

Now, smaller but equally supported events such as Jazz and Poetry on a Stool and other Poetry Slam events receive much attention from the poets and writers who are determined to keep the art alive. Competitions like the Guyana Prize for Literature have also begun to see more participation from younger writers in recent years. In fact, 23-year-old Subraj Singh became the second youngest writer to ever win the Best First Book of Fiction for the 2014 award after Ruel Johnson, who was awarded the Prize in the same category in 2002.

Subraj Singh

The area of visual arts remains relatively silent, with artists with spectacular talents hiding in the shadows due to insufficient means of recognition for their work. Yet, ever so often, we see the awe inducing works of young talented artists through opportunities created by the Guyana National Art Gallery at the Castellani House, and other events such as the Rotaract Club of Central Georgetown's annual Wine and Art event.

Theatre is another area that houses many hidden gems, but which are kept alive through the efforts of the National Cultural Centre and the Theatre Guild. The Guild, which has been in existence since the 1960s, has continually plugged its efforts into the nurturing and training of young artists. Thanks to the Guild and its small but strong society of actors and playwrights, theatre has been kept alive through its productions of plays, workshops, storytelling, music, poetry writing and reading and other artistic endeavours.

If Guyanese artists were not sure before, what has changed now is their attitude and confidence in their work. Their access to information has confirmed for them that what they have to offer is on par with what occurs on the bigger stages, canvases and pages of the world.

What has been given to the young artists is hope, that their work will be recognised, and that Guyana and the talents that spring from it will be seen for the true artistic beauty that has for too long been hidden from the world.

---

*Jasmaine Payne is a freelance writer for the* Guyana Chronicle *newspaper. Photos courtesy of the* Guyana Chronicle

Guyanese literature originates in oral folk tales, legends and creation myths of the First Nations of Guyana, indigenous Arawaks, Macusi and similar Amerindian groups. Rev. W.H. Brett, a missionary among First Nations from 1840 to 1875, was the first to collect Amerindian myths and tales in *Legends and Myths of the Aboriginal Indians of British Guiana* (1880).

The first written examples of Guyanese literature came from British authors who visited Guyana, for instance, *Discoverie of Guiana* (1595) by Sir Walter Raleigh, *Lutchmee and Dilloo* (1877) by Edward Jenkins and *Ninety-Two Days* (1934) by Evelyn Waugh; but the outsider's point of view in these works restricts sympathy for their subject. The first collected local poems and stories appeared from African-Guyanese Egbert Martin in *Leo's Poetical Works* (1883).

Martin, who died from tuberculosis, wrote about the transience of life, employing British technical models, as did other writers whose work can be seen in anthologies such as *Guianese Poetry 1831-1931* (1931), edited by N.E. Cameron; *An Anthology of Poetry by Guianese East Indians* (1934) edited by C.E.J. Ramcharitar Lalla; and *Anthology of Guianese Poetry* (1954) edited by A.J. Seymour (1914-1989). Seymour was productive as a poet, but achieved more for Guyanese literature through critical commentaries and his work as founding editor of the literary journal *Kyk-Over-Al* which lasted from 1945 to 1961, before being re-started in 1984 by Ian McDonald, himself an accomplished poet, novelist and columnist.

By the 1960s, Edgar Mittelholzer (1909-1965), the most fluent and gifted Guyanese novelist, became the first Guyanese author to achieve an international reputation. Mittelholzer produced twenty-eight books in twenty-six years, before he committed suicide. His grandest success being a trilogy of novels: *Children of Kaywana* (1952), *Kaywana Stock* (1954) and *Kaywana Blood* (1958), about descendants of an Amerindian woman from eighteenth-century days of slavery to the 1950s, when Guyana attained universal adult suffrage. This meticulous study of race, colour and class, over the centuries, is without equal in Guyanese fiction.

As a political activist, Guyana's greatest poet, Martin Carter (1927-1997), was jailed for alleged illegal activities in the politically turbulent period of the early 1950s. But his passionate nationalist feeling against British rule – like W.B. Yeats's deep passion for Irish nationalism – inspired some of his most stirring lines, for instance: "I do not sleep to dream, but dream to change the world," in 'Looking at Your Hands'.

With ten novels, including the best documented, fictional portrait available of his coloured, Georgetown, middle class in a trilogy of novels, *From the Heat of the Day* (1979), *One Generation* (1980) and *Genetha* (1981), Roy Heath (1926-2008) is Guyana's finest novelist. He is also versatile as seen in his novel *The Shadow Bride* (1988), which gives an authoritative view of a Hindu Caribbean family, reminiscent of V.S. Naipaul's celebrated *A House for Mr Biswas* (1961). Other distinguished male Guyanese writers are E.R. Braithwaite (b. 1912), a biographer and novelist whose biographical work, *To Sir, With Love* (1959) was made into a successful film in 1967; Denis Williams (1923-1998), novelist and anthropologist; Fred D'Aguiar (b. 1960) novelist, poet and playwright who now lives and teaches in the US; Rupert Roopnaraine (b. 1943) poet, politician, literary critic and art critic; Mark McWatt (b. 1947) poet, story writer, academic and editor; Cyril Dabydeen (b. 1945), prolific writer who lives in Canada and is poet, novelist, editor, story writer and anthologist and Sasenarine Persaud (b. 1958), who lives in the US and writes novels, poems and short stories and David Dabydeen (b. 1955), cousin of Cyril Dabydeen, and probably Guyana's most prolific male author who is an academic

*Guyanese literature can trace its origins back to the folk tales of the nation's indigenous peoples / MED*

poet, novelist, man of letters and former Guyanese ambassador to China.

Of female Guyanese authors, Beryl Gilroy (née Answick 1924-2001), who moved to Britain in 1951, is author of eleven works of fiction and one volume of poems, while Sharon Maas (b. 1951) matches Mittelholzer's fluency and inventiveness in six novels mostly displaying themes on Hindu metaphysics. As partly Indian and Chinese, Janice Shinebourne captures our fullest fictional version of Chinese-Guyanese experience in her novels, while Mahadai Das (1954-2003), perhaps the most promising poet of all, was hampered by illness and misfortune. Ryhaan Shah's *Weaving Water* (2013) is one of the best novels ever written by a Guyanese. Other female Guyanese writers, Grace Nichols (b. 1950), Pauline Melville (b.1948), Brenda DoHarris and Tessa McWatt, illuminate diasporic issues of identity and home.

Authentic speech and manners on Guyanese sugar plantations, re-created in fiction by Rooplall Monar (b. 1945), remind us of frontier-like conditions in Mark Twain's classic novel *The Adventures of Huckleberry Finn* (1884) and confirm them as the truest foundations of local Guyanese culture. But no thumbnail sketch of Guyanese literature can fail to mention Sir Wilson Harris (b.1921), an *eminence grise*, author of two dozen novels, stories, poems and critical essays, and revered for his idiosyncratic mixture of abstract ideas and metaphorical language with notions of illusion and reality, and aboriginal, Amerindian themes.

*Prof Frank Birbalsingh is a pioneering scholar of contemporary Caribbean literature.*

The beautiful lotus lily grows abundantly in the water trenches of Guyana / IB

# A wealth of natural treasures

Guyana is made up of three basic natural regions, which include forests, savannahs and coastal ecosystems.

Forests make up a major part of the Guiana Shield, one of the world's four remaining areas of significant tropical rainforests occupying approximately 75 per cent of Guyana. More than thirty timber species are harvested commercially from these forests, including the greenheart, renowned for its durability. Guyana is the primary source of this wood, since its distribution is mostly limited to this country.

The crabwood tree is also a well-known timber species, as well as the only source of crab oil, which is used to produce soaps, candles and shampoos.

The manicole palm, although not a major wood source, is used to produce 'heart of palm'. This culinary delicacy is canned in Guyana and exported to European markets.

Other tree species provide the raw materials used in the handicraft of Guyana's indigenous Amerindians. These include the fibres from the ite palm and mucru, which are used in weaving and basketry, and the resin from the bulletwood tree, used to sculpt balata ornaments.

Over 5,500 flowering plant species have been collected in Guyana's three natural regions, of which nearly three hundred are found nowhere else on earth. Numerous varieties of heliconias and bromeliads add a splash of vivid colour to the green of the forest and are a regular feature in the local floral industry. Orchids, which account for more than five hundred species, are the largest family in the country and are found in both savannahs and forested areas.

The sedges, grasses and shrubs of the savannahs have developed ingenious ways of coping with the area's seasonal dry spells. These species often have hair-like projections on their leaves, thick stems and root tubers, all serving to trap and store water.

This abundance of plant life provides both the habitat and food to support an amazing variety of indigenous fauna. A diversity of

Yellow banded poison dart frog / DE

Chestnut woodpecker / AS-IIC

The arapaima is one of the world's largest freshwater fish / RA-GTA

Guyana is home to more than 150 species of reptile and amphibian / FN-GTA

Sculpting balata ornaments / KS

Pierid butterflies 'puddling' for minerals / GTA

species includes more than eight hundred species of birds, in excess of two hundred mammal species, over two hundred species of reptiles and amphibians and more than eight hundred species of freshwater fish.

The Iwokrama Rainforest in central Guyana and the Kanuku Mountains in the Rupununi have the highest diversity of bat species ever recorded in the world, with more than ninety of Guyana's 121 species of bats found at each of these two sites. The vast network of waterways of the North Rupununi Floodplain is home to over four hundred species of freshwater fish, the world's highest concentration of species for an area of this size.

Guyana is home to several 'giant' species. Sometimes referred to as the "Giants of El Dorado", these species inhabit the land, sky and water of the remote hinterland and are in most cases threatened or endangered. The 'giants' that stalk the land include the capybara, which can weigh up to 150 pounds and is the largest rodent in the world; the giant anteater which is the largest of this species in the world and the magnificent jaguar which is the largest member of the cat family in the western hemisphere.

There is no shortage of giant reptiles, as the bushmaster is the largest of the pit vipers and the anaconda is one of the biggest snakes in the world. This tendency towards gigantism even extends to invertebrates. Guyana's bird-eating spider is the world's largest, with a 'leg-span' of up to 28 cm (11 in) or the size of a dinner plate.

Not to be outdone, the waterways of the interior are also inhabited by their share of giants. The giant river turtle, arapaima, black caiman and giant otter, are each in their own right, the largest of their species in the world.

Patrolling the skies, the harpy eagle by day and the false vampire bat by night, are both the largest of their kind in the Americas.

From the uppermost reaches of its greenheart forests to the depths of its black caiman-infested rivers, Guyana's flora and fauna are its natural treasures that are beyond compare. Guyana represents a natural refuge of global importance and the challenge is for the country to sustainably benefit from its unique flora and fauna.

*Damian Fernandes*

Capped heron / KL-GTA

# A rewarding birdwatching experience

While Guyana may not have the white-sand beaches that are synonymous with other Caribbean destinations, it does boast an unmatched eco-tourism experience. With more than eight hundred species, from seventy-two different families, birdwatching in Guyana, one of these experiences, is an accessible and enjoyable pastime that offers regular sightings of some of the most sought-after species.

Keen birdwatchers will encounter many key species including those from larger families such as heron; hawk and eagle; falcon and caracara; rail; sandpiper; gull, tern and skimmer; parrot; nighthawk and nightjar; swift; hummingbird; woodpecker; ovenbird; woodcreeper; antbird; tyrant flycatcher; cotinga; finch; and New World blackbird.

Many species can be seen on a daily basis throughout the country, but there are some specific locations that are considered to be ideal for the more complete birdwatching experience. The Iwokrama Centre for Rainforest Conservation and Development boasts around 500 bird species which may be spotted on rivers, in dense rainforests, along the road corridor, or from 100 feet above the forest floor on the Canopy Walkway. Iwokrama is renowned for its numerous fruit-eating birds and many prized species such as the harpy eagle, crimson topaz and the hoatzin (canje pheasant).

Just south of Iwokrama's boundaries is the village of Wowetta, where species such as the Guianan cock-of-the-rock, red and green macaw, golden-handed manakin, toucanette, capuchin bird, green oropendola, rufous-winged ground cuckoo and black curacao can be seen.

Karanambu Ranch is well-known for the work of its owner, Diane McTurk, in the rehabilitation of orphaned giant river otters. However, birdwatchers have been flocking there for many years to see some of the more than three hundred species of bird supported by the Rupununi River and nearby wetlands. Highlights include the jabiru stork, tyrant manakins, capuchinbird, bearded tachuri, green ibis and rufescent heron.

Further south, in the Rupununi, is the famed Dadanawa Ranch. Here, birdwatchers can head-out on horseback to look for harpy eagle nests, Guianan cock-of-the-rock and the rare red siskin.

Other popular birding destinations include Kaieteur Falls, which offers the spectacular sight of thousands of white-collared swifts that nest behind the falls. Shanklands Rainforest Resort on the Essequibo River is prized for accessible birdwatching of species such as the tropical kingbird, swallow-winged puffbird, common tody-flycatcher, red-bellied toucan, violaceous trogon and white-plumed antbird.

The nation's capital is, itself, home to more than two hundred species of bird as well as the Guyana Amazon Tropical Birding Society (GATBS). The organisation runs trips to nearby birding locations such as the Botanic Gardens and the Promenade Gardens where it is not uncommon to see upwards of fifty species in just a few hours.

---

*Kirk Smock is a freelance writer and tourism consultant from the United States. His acclaimed guide,* Guyana *(Bradt Travel Guides), is in its second edition.*

The hoatzin or Canje pheasant / RJF

Guianan cock-of-the-rock / KL-GTA

The Amazon is home to the the largest and most diverse tropical rainforest on the planet. As 'the lungs of the earth', they provide many essential services including the removal of 1.2 billion tonnes of carbon dioxide per year and replacing it with oxygen / FN-GTA

# Iwokrama – A model for the world

Every day we hear about the ill effects of climate change, global warming and greenhouse gases. To help, we are advised to drive less, fly less and turn down the air-conditioning and heat. The new United Nations Sustainable Development Goals and the UN Conference on Climate Change, COP 21, held in Paris in December 2015, both include sustainable forest management goals as a priority. Yet the money is slow to follow the rhetoric and we hear little of the importance of rainforests in this fight - this is why, by the time you have finished reading this article, another 600 acres of rainforest would have been lost globally.

### THE CHALLENGE
Rainforest destruction is driven by increasing demands for immediate profit – for valuable 'cash crops' such as timber, soya, bio-fuels and beef. Traditional financial values too often overshadow the 'softer' and less quantified ecological values. Yet the financial value of a standing forest is real and can be quantified.

Rainforests are global utilities and the 'lungs of the earth' providing many services to human-kind from removing and storing 1.2 billion tonnes of carbon dioxide per year to providing fresh water for agriculture. They are usually located in some of the poorest geographies in the world – the irony is that the poverty can easily be alleviated by razing those same forests and so there is always a battle in these areas between short-term gains versus long-term thinking.

### THE SOLUTION
Global carbon emissions levels are at 400 ppm (parts per million) and the upper threshold of tolerance is believed to be 450 ppm, so there may be only a decade or two left before our planet reaches the point of no return. Rainforest destruction is accelerating this process.

We must therefore seek to reduce our emissions dramatically and one such way is to save the remaining rainforests by understanding the critical eco-system services

Accommodation at the Iwokrama River Lodge / DW-GTA

The harpy eagle is the largest and most powerful raptor found in the Americas and is among the largest eagles in the world / KL-GTA

The illusive jaguar is Guyana's national animal / IB

Giant river otter / IIC

Spectacled caiman / DW-GTA

they deliver and by creating innovative models that demonstrate the substantive financial value of these rainforests.

We pay for electricity, gas, oil, water and waste services but nothing for rainforest services on which we all depend. How can we capture and quantify this value? How do we turn these rich forests into long-term capital assets, not short-term expendable commodities?

THE IWOKRAMA MODEL
There is one such global utility nestled deep in central Guyana – the 371,000 ha (1,000,000 acre) Iwokrama Forest, home to the Macushi indigenous nation and some of the richest biodiversity in the region.

The Iwokrama International Centre (IIC) was established in 1996 to manage the Iwokrama Forest and it is part of the Guiana Shield ecosystem which borders the Amazon and dedicated by an enlightened Guyanese Government to its people, to the Commonwealth and to the wider international community for international research into sustainable development, climate change and global warming.

The Iwokrama forest and its research centre are unique, providing a dedicated environment and bringing together people, science and business to test the concept of a truly sustainable forest, where conservation, environmental balance and economic use are mutually reinforcing. The forest is very well studied, documented and managed with a complex zoning exercise which split the forest equally into a Sustainable Use Area (SUA) and Wilderness Preserve (WP). It is managed using a comprehensive management plan coupled with a state-of-the-art Geographic Information Systems (GIS).

*Natural Assets*. The Iwokrama Forest and the neighbouring North Rupununi wetlands are an extraordinary ecosystem with healthy

The Iwokrama Canopy Walkway is the only one of its kind in the Guiana Sheild. It is 100 feet (33 metres) above the rainforest floor and has four platforms offering spectacular views and unrivalled birdwatching opportunities / GTA

populations of some of the world's largest and most endangered species – including the 'Giants of El Dorado' including the harpy eagle, the jaguar and the giant anteater. It hosts the largest number of fish and bat species in the world for an area of its size. Faunal diversity also includes 30 per cent of which is classified as rare and endangered, more than 130 species of mammals; more than 500 species of birds; over 150 species of reptiles and amphibians; 420 species of fish and 86 species of bats.

What is also impressive about the range and diversity of animals found in the Iwokrama Forest is that it accounts for almost half of all the animal species found in the whole of Guyana. Even more noteworthy is that when those species are combined with those found in the adjacent Rupununi Wetlands, they account for almost three-quarters of all the animal species found in Guyana.

Floral diversity includes nine distinct forest types with the largest being mixed greenheart forest. Botanical surveys of the Iwokrama Forest have found over 1,250 (out of an estimated 2,000) species of plants.

**The work of the IIC**. The Iwokrama International Centre, along with the Government of Guyana, the Commonwealth Secretariat, the local communities and other partners, is developing new models that demonstrate the value of rainforests so as to enable countries with rainforests to earn significant income from the sustainable use of forest resources and eco-system services whilst at the same time employing innovative conservation practices.

Some of the business models being developed will also help offset Iwokrama's core costs and include:

*Selective timber harvesting* – Iwokrama is developing Phase II of its low impact sustainable forestry model which is in the process of being fully certified by the Forest Stewardship Council (FSC). Typically, just five to six mature trees per hectare are taken every sixty years and only from a small part of the forest;

*Eco-tourism* – rainforest bird watching is very popular and Iwokrama continues to develop facilities; currently it has 20 kilometres of forest trails. The Canopy Walkway, Turtle Mountain hike and nocturnal animal spotting activities are also popular among the 1,200

The red howler monkey is native to South and Central America. Its distinct and loud howl can be heard across many miles of rainforest / IIC

Toco toucan / CC-GTA

Guyana is home to more than 150 species of reptile and amphibian / FN-GTA

Amazonian royal flycatcher / TH-IIC

tourists who visit Iwokrama annually. See www.iwokramariverlodge.com for more information;

*Learning services* – the Iwokrama International Centre provides training for others involved in rainforest management elsewhere in South America and beyond. It also attracts students from international universities and education institutions to study the forest;

*Eco-system Services (ESS)* – the IIC developed Guyana's first ESS arrangement in 2008 and is now working on a new initiative where REDD+ arrangements for reducing emissions from deforestation and forest degradation can be implemented alongside sustainable use activities. The aim is to pioneer financial instruments based on the utility value of the eco-system services of the forest - rain generation, biodiversity, and soil and carbon conservation. It is intended to go beyond simple eco-philanthropy and establish that projects backed by natural assets are bankable propositions.

These models provide fertile ground for a robust research, science and monitoring programme manned by visiting and local scientists, students, interns and volunteers. They also provide support to the twenty local indigenous communities under the umbrella of the North Rupununi District Development Board (NRDDB), all of whom have a stake in the commercial activities of the IIC with direct cash payments, as well as other benefits, including capacity building and the employment they offer. These communities are integral partners in the management of the Iwokrama Forest and the Centre has complex agreements including a Collaborative Management Agreement and Memorandum of Understanding with them.

The orange-winged parrot is one of over five hundred species or bird found in Guyana / FN-GTA

Turu Falls area in the Iwokrama Forest in central Guyana / RT-IIC

## USE IT WISELY OR LOSE IT

Rainforests are located primarily in some of the world's poorest countries so the forest capital *must* generate income, which benefits their economies and societies more than the temptation to allow other less preferred development instead.

If the global community, increasingly aware of the impact of climate change, wants tropical forests to survive, the services of the rainforest can no longer go unrecognised or unpaid. Iwokrama's pioneering solution could pave the way for sustainable and innovative sources of finance on a wider scale to match a new global priority of national ownership and local stewardship.

Applied widely, Iwokrama's model for rainforest management could help reduce the destruction of rainforests and create momentum for a new international valuation and market for natural assets and eco-system payments.

## THE FUTURE

Against the background of a failing international economy, which forces policy and money-makers to prioritise short-term profits and policies instead of longer term and greener growth strategies, the immediate dilemma is how to persuade investors and these international policy makers to recognise the immense values forests contain, invest in them and design frameworks to regulate their trade.

But climate change waits for no one - the Arctic ice cap continues to shrink and the degradation of rainforest assets continues unabated, wreaking havoc on the forest peoples and the national economies that depend on them. How to inspire investors and decision makers to overcome their hesitation is an urgent task for the IIC and its partners.

After twenty years, Iwokrama's work and models are still relevant and key in this pursuit and we need to encourage those that can make a difference to realise that they must be involved in supporting its work and that they too can be pathfinders, showing others that by investing a little now we can avoid a bigger bill for everyone later. To succeed, we have to communicate the real value of an asset that is as yet unrealised. There is much hard work ahead.

*Dane Gobin is Chief Executive Officer at the Iwokrama International Centre*

The iconic Kaieteur Falls is located within the Kaieteur National Park and is Guyana's leading tourist attraction. The park was established in 1929 to preserve and protect the natural scenery as well as the flora and fauna / IB

# Fifty years of tourism – Guyana's golden opportunity

The tourism story of Guyana can truthfully be described as a journey from obscurity to prominence; from the shadows to the limelight. The celebration of the 50th year of Guyana's Independence is a fitting stimulus for reflection upon the progress of the tourism industry in Guyana since independence. That journey to prominence was never a linear, unbroken movement, but a winding road that saw fitful and intermittent bursts interspersed with pauses and stops.

When one considers the legacy of official indifference, even hostility in some quarters, towards the development of tourism in Guyana, the evolution of tourism to its present prominence must be regarded as no small miracle. The decade after the attainment of Independence ushered in that formidable industrial trinity of sugar, rice and bauxite that became the backbone of the Guyana economy. The dominance of that trinity meant that there was little incentive to pit Guyana's dark waters against the azure waters that washed the shores of the Caribbean as part of any scheme for tourism development.

In addition, at least one former President (Forbes Burnham) harboured reservations about the social impact of tourism upon the population, post-independence, and cautioned about the propensity of tourism to inculcate what he termed "false values". Another former President (Cheddi Jagan) remarked, in a personal interview with the author, that given the economic dominance of sugar, rice and bauxite, his government saw little need to venture into tourism.

Therefore, the Golden Arrowhead was being hoisted against a national backdrop of official lukewarm-ness towards and suspicion about the development of tourism. At this time too, the strength of the dominant image of Caribbean tourism – blue waters and white sands – made many in Guyana feel that the country was not in the same tourism league as its counterparts in the Caribbean island chain.

The reality is that in spite of the official coolness towards tourism development in Guyana in the immediate post-Independence period, and despite the widespread perception

Located a few miles from the capital, Ogle International Airport is the main domestic hub for passenger and cargo transport primarily between Georgetown and Guyana's hinterland, including Kaieteur National Park / IB

Maipaima Eco-Lodge is nestled within the foothills of the Kanuku mountains in the south-west / KS-GTA

Air Services Ltd operates flights from Ogle Airport to Kaieteur Falls / KA

The rooftop Aura bar at the Pegasus Hotel in Georgetown

Kurupukari rapids in central Guyana /LH-IIC

that Guyana was a country off the beaten Caribbean tourist track, Guyana had a reputation for being a place of wild and haunting beauty. This fascination with Guyana is largely a story of travels in the interior; trips undertaken as early as the last decades of the nineteenth century by colonial officials (who had the means to undertake such journeys) tired of the city and needing to escape the confines of the plantation.

One such famous visitor, geologist and government surveyor was Charles Barrington Brown, reputed to be the first European to have sighted Kaieteur Falls in April 1870. For Barrington Brown the encounter with the Kaieteur Falls was a near mystical experience which he captured and expressed in language that borders upon religious utterance. Further, such description epitomises the reaction of many visitors to the sights, landscapes, flora and fauna that Guyana offers. This is the essence of the golden opportunity that tourism holds for Guyana – the jewel that sits on the north-eastern shoulder of South America. Welcome to Amazon country!

Guyana regards all of its territory as Amazon territory and the country is described in tourism promotions as 'the Amazon adventure' and as 'South America undiscovered' (current slogan). These slogans, far from being mere decorative descriptions, announce and define a national identity – South American/Amazonian – that places us, from a tourism standpoint, more among the family of South American than among the Caribbean countries.

The Amazon adventure is a counterpoint and complement to the dominant image of tourism in the Caribbean.

'South America undiscovered' is an invitation to undertake journeys up spectacular black water creeks and rivers; it is an invocation of ancient cultures practised by peoples proud of their origins.

Grand Coastal Hotel at Le Ressouvenir, East Coast Demerara, offers high quality accommodation and dining / IB

Herdmanston Lodge in Georgetown / KJ

Rainforest B&B in Georgetown offers a more bohemian bed and breakfast experience / KJ

Nestled among the trees, the Pandama Retreat is a rustic sanctuary and is ideal for eco-tourists / KJ

'South America undiscovered' is Guyana's assertion and reiteration of its continental destiny. That assertion is based upon a number of policy directions, among which is its national tourism strategy principally aimed at driving tourism based upon its land and water resources – essentially the world of the Amazon.

Much of the excitement that inheres in the Guyana tourism product is water-based. Experiences of the Kaieteur Falls, Orinduik Falls, the waters of the Essequibo and the myriad rivers, lakes and creeks are like an Amazonia baptism for visitors.

These dark waters hold a special enchantment for travellers looking for a different experience.

Region 7, for example, in the Mazaruni Potaro, rivers support yachting, regattas and recreation in what is known as the Bartica triangle.

Farther north, Shell Beach abuts the mighty Atlantic Ocean as it plays host to the varieties of nesting turtles.

The waters of the Kamuni Creek in Demerara are sheltered for much of its course by an arch that forms overhead as the creek drifts past the odd, isolated dwelling hut, or has its waters disturbed by the small outboard motor boat ferrying a family out to the open waters of the Demerara river.

Quite apart from the aesthetic quality of Guyana's Amazonia waters, they are also home

The Moruca River is in the Barima-Waini region of northern Guyana / GTA

to intriguing varieties of fish that make them a sport fisher's dream. The waters are famous for bass, Haimara, Leukanani, Arowana, Payara, Hyera, Mullet, Catfish, Gilbaker, Tiger fish, Lau-lau, Pacu and other species.

These are the waters of Amazonia yielding an abundance of fish life. The legendary arapaima, the largest fresh water fish, swims in the waters of Guyana, while in the Rupununi sea otters belch out their idiosyncratic welcome.

Guyana's landscapes often inspire the mood of William Wordsworth who, in 1802, composed the famous line, "Earth hath not anything to show more fair" as he stood upon Westminster Bridge and gazed upon "a sight so touching in its majesty". In Guyana those sights abound as its Amazonia topography manifests rolling savannahs, suddenly interrupted, as in the Rupununi, by the imposing Kanukus.

The more daring and adventurous travellers may even feel inspired to conquer Guyana's highest peak, Mount Roraima, while the more conservative may be content to observe, on and behind the coastlands, that intriguing mix of creek, river, forest and flat plains. As is the case where such varied topography exists, biodiversity flourishes. Guyana is no exception, with its cornucopia of plants, flowers, trees, animals, insects and birds.

As Guyana celebrates 50 years of Independence and looks back upon its tourism journey, there is reason to celebrate and sufficient incentive to exploit the golden opportunity that its Amazonia territory presents.

*Donald Sinclair is Director General in Guyana's Ministry of Tourism*

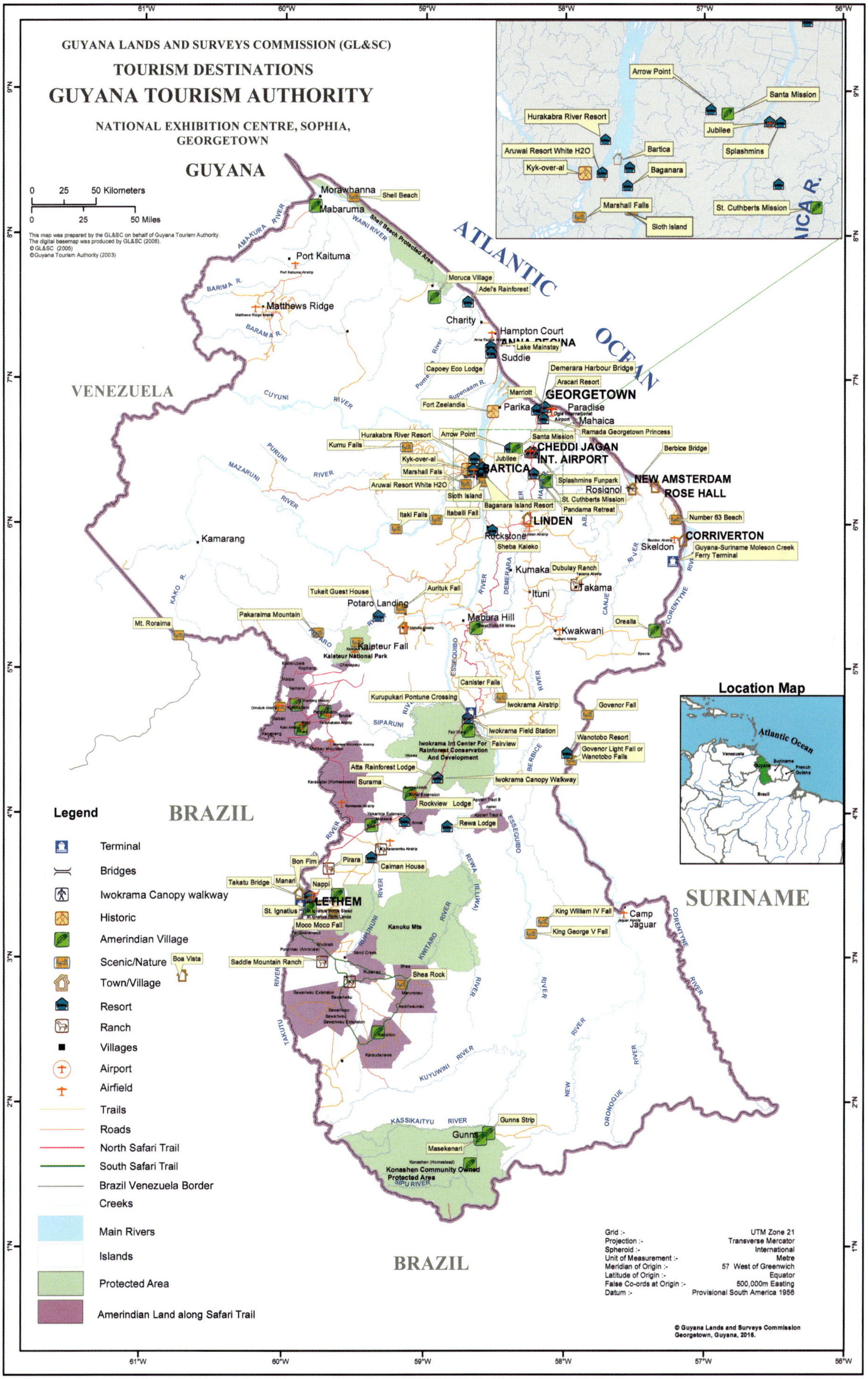
GUYANA LANDS AND SURVEYS COMMISSION (GL&SC)
TOURISM DESTINATIONS
GUYANA TOURISM AUTHORITY
NATIONAL EXHIBITION CENTRE, SOPHIA, GEORGETOWN
GUYANA
0 25 50 Kilometers
0 25 50 Miles
This map was prepared by the GL&SC on behalf of Guyana Tourism Authority.
The digital basemap was produced by GL&SC (2005).
©GL&SC (2005)
©Guyana Tourism Authority (2003)
VENEZUELA
BRAZIL
SURINAME
ATLANTIC OCEAN
Location Map
Atlantic Ocean
Legend
Terminal
Bridges
Iwokrama Canopy walkway
Historic
Amerindian Village
Scenic/Nature
Boa Vista
Town/Village
Resort
Ranch
Villages
Airport
Airfield
Trails
Roads
North Safari Trail
South Safari Trail
Brazil Venezuela Border
Creeks
Main Rivers
Islands
Protected Area
Amerindian Land along Safari Trail
Arrow Point
Santa Mission
Hurakabra River Resort
Jubilee
Aruwai Resort White H2O
Bartica
Splashmins
Kyk-over-al
Baganara
Marshall Falls
St. Cuthberts Mission
Sloth Island
Morawhanna
Shell Beach
Mabaruma
Port Kaituma
Matthews Ridge
Moruca Village
Adel's Rainforest
Charity
Hampton Court
Lake Mainstay
Suddie
Capoey Eco Lodge
Demerara Harbour Bridge
Aracari Resort
Marriott
GEORGETOWN
Fort Zeelandia
Parika
Paradise
Mahaica
Ramada Georgetown Princess
Hurakabra River Resort
Arrow Point
Santa Mission
Kumu Falls
CHEDDI JAGAN INT. AIRPORT
Berbice Bridge
Kyk-over-al
Jubilee
BARTICA
Marshall Falls
Aruwai Resort White H2O
Splashmins Funpark
NEW AMSTERDAM
Rosignol
ROSE HALL
Sloth Island
St. Cuthberts Mission
Baganara Island Resort
Pandama Retreat
Itaki Falls
Itaballi Fall
LINDEN
Number 63 Beach
Rockstone
CORRIVERTON
Skeldon
Sheba Kaieko
Guyana-Suriname Moleson Creek Ferry Terminal
Kamarang
Kumaka
Dubulay Ranch
Takama
Ituni
Tukeit Guest House
Aurituk Fall
Potaro Landing
Pakaraima Mountain
Mabura Hill
Orealla
Mt. Roraima
Kwakwani
Kaieteur Fall
Kaieteur National Park
Canister Falls
Kurupukari Pontune Crossing
Iwokrama Airstrip
Govenor Fall
Iwokrama Field Station
Wanotobo Resort
Iwokrama Int Center For Rainforest Conservation And Development
Fairview
Govenor Light Fall or Wanotobo Falls
Atta Rainforest Lodge
Surama
Iwokrama Canopy Walkway
Rockview Lodge
Rewa Lodge
Bon Fim
Pirara
Caiman House
Takatu Bridge
Manari
Nappi
LETHEM
St. Ignatius
Moco Moco Fall
Kanuku Mts
King William IV Fall
Camp Jaguar
King George V Fall
Saddle Mountain Ranch
Shea Rock
Gunns Strip
Gunns
Masekenari
Konashen Community Owned Protected Area
CUYUNI RIVER
MAZARUNI RIVER
PURUNI RIVER
SIPARUNI
ESSEQUIBO
DEMERARA RIVER
BERBICE RIVER
CORENTYNE RIVER
RUPUNUNI RIVER
TAKUTU
KUYUWINI RIVER
KASSIKAITYU RIVER
NEW RIVER
KWITARO RIVER
REWA (ILLIWA)
Grid :- UTM Zone 21
Projection :- Transverse Mercator
Spheroid :- International
Unit of Measurement :- Metre
Meridian of Origin :- 57 West of Greenwich
Latitude of Origin :- Equator
False Co-ords at Origin :- 500,000m Easting
Datum :- Provisional South America 1956
© Guyana Lands and Surveys Commission Georgetown, Guyana, 2016.

Potaro River viewed from the crest of Kaieteur Falls. The river runs for 140 miles before flowing into the Essequibo River. Kaieteur Falls is the most notable of nine waterfalls on the Potaro River / IB

# Rivers and water lores

Guyana is crisscrossed by 1,613 named creeks and 1,515 named rivers. The four largest rivers are the Berbice, Demerara, Essequibo and Corentyne. Each creek or river has some association with legends, myths and local tales and are acknowledged as essential to the green heart of the nation.

A literary journey through these numerous waterways is as exciting and educational as a physical trip.

All the rivers originate in the sparsely populated highlands, south of the country, running in a northerly direction towards a densely populated coastland to empty themselves into the Atlantic Ocean. They give and sustain life and provide a nexus for many communities and cities.

**Essequibo River**

The Essequibo is the largest river in Guyana and runs for over 600 miles from its source in the Kamoa Mountains to its mouth which is about 20 miles in width. The river flows through some 365 islands of which Wakenaan, Leguan and Hogg islands are the most populated and developed.

The Essequibo is fed by many tributaries on which are located Guyana's more well-known waterfalls, the most notable of which being Kaieteur Falls, located on the Potaro River.

**Demerara River**

The Demerara River flows for more than 200 miles from its source to enter into the Atlantic Ocean at its estuary in Georgetown. 'Demerara' originated from the Arawak word 'malali' meaning 'fast moving stream'.

As well as flowing past the nation's capital, the river encompasses the island of Borselem, capital of the former colony of Demerara during the Dutch occupation.

**Berbice River**

The Berbice River is 370 miles long and falls within the ancient county of Berbice. 'Berbice' is a derivative of the Arawak word 'beribishi', a type of banana that grew wild on its banks.

The main tributary of the Berbice River is the Canje Creek. Here, between these two water systems, you can ponder the events of the 1763 Berbice Slave Uprising.

**Corentyne River**

The eastern most of Guyana's waterways is the Corentyne River which flows approximately 475 miles from its source in the Akarai Mountains. It forms a boundary with neighbouring Suriname.

## WATER LORES

There are many tales and stories linked to each waterway; linked to its name, to events that unfolded and to its navigability and functional roles.

Essequibo, for example, is a combination of two Arawak words, 'dishiki', meaning fireside, and 'abo' forming the word 'dishikibo'. It is believed that, because the river was so wide and difficult to cross, travellers were forced to carry a 'fireside' in order to cook food.

These lores, like Water-mama and Massacouraman, were never substantiated but grew with every embellished retelling. It is the teller, the weaver of stories, who lends credence to the folklore of Guyana's many waters.

When the teller describes the 'fair maid' (water-mama or mermaid) whose upper body is perfectly formed, graced with creamy skin and with long blond hair, reposing in a deserted waterway on a large rock combing her tresses with a golden or silver comb, you're sure to fall in love with her.

Depending on her mood, she may turn fully woman, losing her elegant fishtail, able to delight you with her sumptuous gifts. Or she may offer you untold riches which go to your head causing you to break your promise of secrecy to her. Your end: a broken neck.

The 'Massacouraman' inhabits the menacing dark waters of the hinterland and is a male human-like, hairy monster of the water, forever in contact with the water in isolated places. When he is angry - which is always - he tears out human hearts or he takes the victim under the sinister black waters. He is not beguiling but menacing and raucous; his intention is clear, so stay clear of him.

The best known water-lore of Guyana is *'if yuh drink creek wata and eat labba, yuh boun foh cum baak'*.

*Petamber Persaud*

The inland waterways are a vital and often busy transport network for Guyana's indigenous communities / DH-GTA

183

## Painting the wind – A personal reflection

When I travel up the Essequibo I feel I touch an immortal world. Today I recall what I once expressed when, not for the first time, the river clarified life's daily problems and concerns into a true perspective.

I have no purpose other than to say there is great beauty in this world and that it gives me pleasure to try to express it and that it is especially good to know that in Guyana such beauty is near at hand. We dash from moment to moment without reflection but we should halt and sometimes spend a different sort of time.

Every so often I go with my family up the Essequibo for an unforgettable, life-enhancing few days. We stay in a small and lovely house, whose ownership we share with friends, embowered in the green forest set on a niche of bright sand on the edge of the great river. The peace and beauty of this perfect place cannot be imagined, it can only be experienced. Friends, seasoned travellers around this multi-marvelled earth, who have been there with us have said they know of nowhere which excels, and very few which equal, this place in its unique, uncorrupted loveliness.

There is boating and swimming and wave-running and expeditions near and far and forest ventures and parties in other river-homes. But I care these days simply to spend the time sitting and reading, watching the river change and the sky grow light then luminous then dark again and then watch the astonishing splendour of the stars at night. Storms come and go and they toss the river as if it were the sea. I love the storms. And by now I have seen scores upon scores of dawns and dusks and not one is the same in how they colour the sky and the river that is more like a sea where that bright beach and green forest curves. I have seen more colours there than scientists say exist. I remember once on two successive days there was a dawn so explosively red it seemed a volcano had burst, followed by one whose sky was silver-pale and veined with lightest blue. One evening on a recent visit huge, leaden-coloured, ominous clouds hung over the house. I had just read a poem which described a sky "the colour of the desperation of wolves" and as I looked up at those clouds about to fall on us I knew what the poet meant.

I find there long hours of slow-moving time to read. Is there anything better, more soul-satisfying, at my age anyway, than an amplitude of time, with no commitments in prospect, no business to transact, to read books you have looked forward to reading, saved up for the right interval of unoccupied hours, treasuring the thought? This is not a mere reading of books, it is the long-drawn-out savouring of one of the great pleasures of life. I find a place in the shade of a tree by the river-rocks on the beach and set down a comfortable chair and ahead of me stretch as many hours as I like for the enjoyment of books and the pleasures of reflection.

I read the pages more slowly than usual, often turning back to re-read passages because their beauty or relevance registers with special impact in retrospect as the book progresses or simply because some expression of an insight is so remarkable that I want to remind myself more than once of how it has been written. Often also my eyes lift off the page simply to look at the great river and the immense sky which arches over it to see with ever-renewed wonder how their moods and patterns everlastingly change and I think how each moment is unique and eternal. Sudden shifts of wind or cloud-shadow change the texture of the water from brocade to silk to satin to rough cotton. Progress with my book is slow. But why should I worry about that? There is no need to hurry. There are no deadlines. As it gets too dark to read I set aside my book and look up at the stars.

Night after night I have sat beneath the stars on the bank of the great Essequibo and have been for hours wrapped in wonder. Here at night the stars are as big as in Van Gogh's mad skies. They burn with a wild freedom you do not see

"Nowhere else on earth could there be a better place to be a great painter or a great photographer" / GTA

in town. Gradually a feeling of exultation and an expansion of the mind takes hold which is hard to explain. There is an essay by the 18th. Century Englishman, Joseph Addison, entitled 'On the Pleasures of the Imagination' which has a passage which comes near what I have felt many nights up the Essequibo:

> *"We are filled with a pleasing astonishment, to see so many worlds, hanging one above another, and sliding round their axles in such an amazing pomp and solemnity. If, after this, we contemplate those wild fields of ether, that reach in height as far as from Saturn to the fixed stars, and run abroad almost to an infinitude, our imagination finds its capacity filled with so immense a prospect, and puts itself upon the stretch to comprehend it. But if we rise yet higher, and consider the fixed stars as so many vast oceans of flame, that are each of them attended with a different set of planets, and still discover new firmaments and new lights that are sunk further into those unfathomable depths of ether, so as not to be seen by the strongest of our telescopes, we are lost in such a labyrinth of suns and worlds, and confounded with the immensity and magnificence of nature."*

Nowhere else on earth could there be a better place to be a great painter or a great photographer. Up the Essequibo I have wished so often that I possessed the art of a Ron Savory or a Bobby Fernandes to do justice to the infinite beauty of the changing sky and river scenes and forest in the wind. Horace in his treatise *Ars Poetica* wrote that poetry should reproduce the qualities of painting and more than anywhere where I have tried to write poetry it is by the Essequibo I have felt the truth that all art is one and takes at such times a powerful cue from nature.

There are days on the Essequibo of brooding clouds, filled with thunder, and brewing squalls and lashing rain-storms marching up the immense reaches of the river, followed so often by a serene calmness in the air, when I have so deeply felt what soul-satisfaction it would give to be able to paint the wind. If ever there was wind that deserved to be painted it is Essequibo wind, how it moves the caravans of clouds, how it roughs up the shining coat of the evening-water, how it makes a green tumult in the crowns of the forest trees, how the birds ride the heavens on it. Please God, if I am born again with the powers of an artist, let me go again to the Essequibo and read the books I love and this time paint the wind.

*Ian McDonald is a celebrated Caribbean writer who describes himself as "Antiguan by ancestry, Trinidadian by birth, Guyanese by adoption and West Indian by conviction."*

## Roads and Trails

Just before British Guiana became independent, the country was meagrely endowed with roads and trails. There was a coastal road system between the Pomeroon River and the Corentyne River; roads on either bank of the Demerara River – the one on the eastern bank connecting Georgetown with the main airport, and the one on the western bank connecting Vreed en Hoop with the Wales Sugar Estate. In addition to these 300 km of roadway, there were another forty or so tentatively creeping a few kilometres up the banks of some of the more important rivers.

There was also the 'cattle trail', but this was accessible only by cattle, men on horseback and 'droghers'.

After independence, the need for the accelerated development of vehicular access to the hinterland and borders was acknowledged and the coastal road system was drastically upgraded. The first major initiative to further the conquering of the hinterland was launched with the completion of the Soesdyke-Linden 'highway'. By the early 1990s, a 300 km laterite ('red' soil) surfaced driving route had been established from Linden to the south-western border with Brazil. Forestry initiatives with a German company at Mabura in the south and with a Malaysian company in the north-west made a huge impact on the expansion of the hinterland's vehicular access network.

Several factors contributed to the further rapid development of a hinterland road network in the last twenty-five years. These included the progressive decline of the sugar industry coupled with the rise of the price of gold and forest products. By 2005, with the price of gold rising on the world market and remaining at a sustainable high for nearly a decade, the hinterland network was guaranteed. Currently, it is estimated that the total length of roads and accessible vehicular trails in Guyana is in excess of 5000 km. If the country proceeds with its intention to establish and institutionally strengthen towns in each region and to proceed with the accelerated population of its western border for purposes of security, one could anticipate a doubling of this inventory over the next decade.   *Terrence Fletcher*

Pictured: Georgetown to Lethem by mini-bus is a 550km journey that takes around 16 hours during the dry season / IB

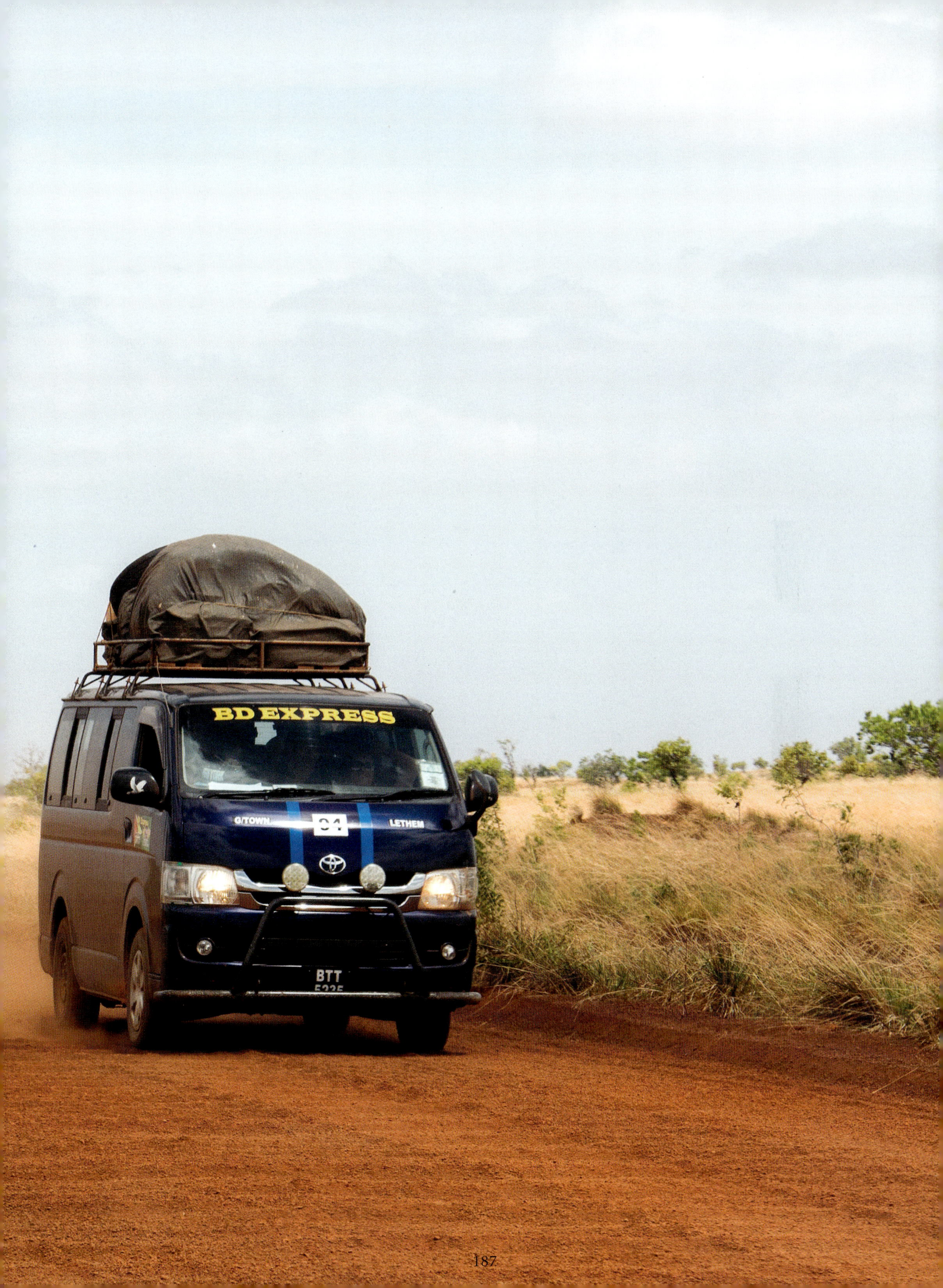
BD EXPRESS
G/TOWN
LETHEM
BTT

Guyana from Above

*A rare view of the spectacular Kaieteur Falls / IB*

Guyana from Above

The view from the town of Vreed en Hoop, left, across the mouth of the Demerara River to Georgetown / IB

Guyana from Above

Opened in 1978, the Demerara Harbour Bridge was built to last for ten years but, after nearly forty years, it is still in service / IB

Guyana from Above

The Georgetown docks and ferry stelling on the banks of the Demerara river overlooking Stabroek Market and the busy capital city / IB

# Guyana from Above

Stabroek Market, and the streets around it, is a vital hub within Guyana's busy capital / IB

The Sea Wall in Georgetown is a popular thoroughfare for walkers, joggers and cyclists / IB / IB

The Ramada Georgetown Princess Hotel in Providence, East Bank Demerara / IB

National Aquatic Centre in Liliendaal / IB

Guyana from Above

Cheddi Jagan International Airport (formerly Timehri International Airport) has two runways and the terminal has six ground-level passenger gates. The airport is twenty-five miles south of the capital on the east bank of the Demerara River / IB

Guyana from Above

Burning sugar cane fields prior to harvesting / IB

Guyana from Above

The town of Parika, and its busy ferry stelling, is located at the mouth of the Essequibo River on the eastern bank. Scheduled ferry services and river taxis (speedboats) provide connections to and from Parika and Leguan Island, Supenaam, Bartica, Adventure, Wakenaam Island and Hog Island / IB

Guyana from Above

Seen from the air, the moorings at Parika ferry stelling show that Guyana is a land of many boats as well as a land of many waters / IB

Guyana from Above

Mon Repos in the Demerara-Mahaica region (Region 4) / IB

# Guyana from Above

A network of irrigation and drainage canals runs throughout Guyana's coastal plain / IB

# Guyana from Above

Canal Number One / IB

Guyana from Above

Located in Georgetown, Le Repentir Cemetery is one of the largest in the Caribbean. Its name dates back over two hundred and fifty years when the site was part of a sugar estate owned by Pierre Louis de Saffon. Born in France in 1724, he escaped into exile in what was then the Dutch colony of Demerara, now Guyana. His exile followed a duel with his brother, whom he killed; duelling had been banned in France since the early 17th century. In Demerara, he was a penitent exile and later became a wealthy sugar planter. His sorrow over having killed his brother was reflected in the naming of three of his estates – Le Repentir (repentance), La Penitence (penitence) and Le Misere (misery). He died in 1784.

La Penitence is now a borough of Georgetown through which runs Saffon Street. A monument to Pierre Louis de Saffon, marking his place of burial, is located in the churchyard of Saint Saviour's Anglican Church on Broad and Saffon Streets. Le Misere no longer exists in name / IB

Guyana from Above

Located on the Demerara River in Region 9, the bauxite mining town of Linden is Guyana's second largest town after Georgetown. It includes the communities of Mackenzie and Wismar which are connected by the Mackenzie-Wismar Bridge / IB

# Guyana from Above

A bird's eye view of Kaieteur Falls as seen from one of the regular flights to and from Guyana's iconic national treasure / IB

The Berbice River Bridge connects the east bank at Crab Island to the west bank at D'Edward Village. The floating pontoon bridge is almost one mile long and has a retractable central section to allow marine traffic to pass up and down the river. The bridge is tolled and was open to the public on Christmas Eve in 2008. Opened thirty years after the Demerara Harbour Bridge, the two bridges connect the regions of Essequibo, Demerara and Berbice with good quality, all-weather roads / IB

Opened in 1978, Canje Bridge in East Berbice-Corentyne (Region 6) was built to replace the original swing bridge which had been in service since 1891 / IB

Rice mill: Rice production, along with sugar, dominates Guyana's agricultural industry. Most of the rice is consumed locally but significant quantities are exported to Venezuela and other parts of the Caribbean / IB

Guyana from Above

Located at the south-western border, the Takutu River Bridge links Lethem in Guyana to Bonfim in Brazil. Opened in 2009, the bridge is a rare example of a land border where drivers must change from driving on the left in Guyana to driving on the right in Brazil. This changeover is achieved by means of a crossover road in Guyana. Lethem is pictured in the background / IB

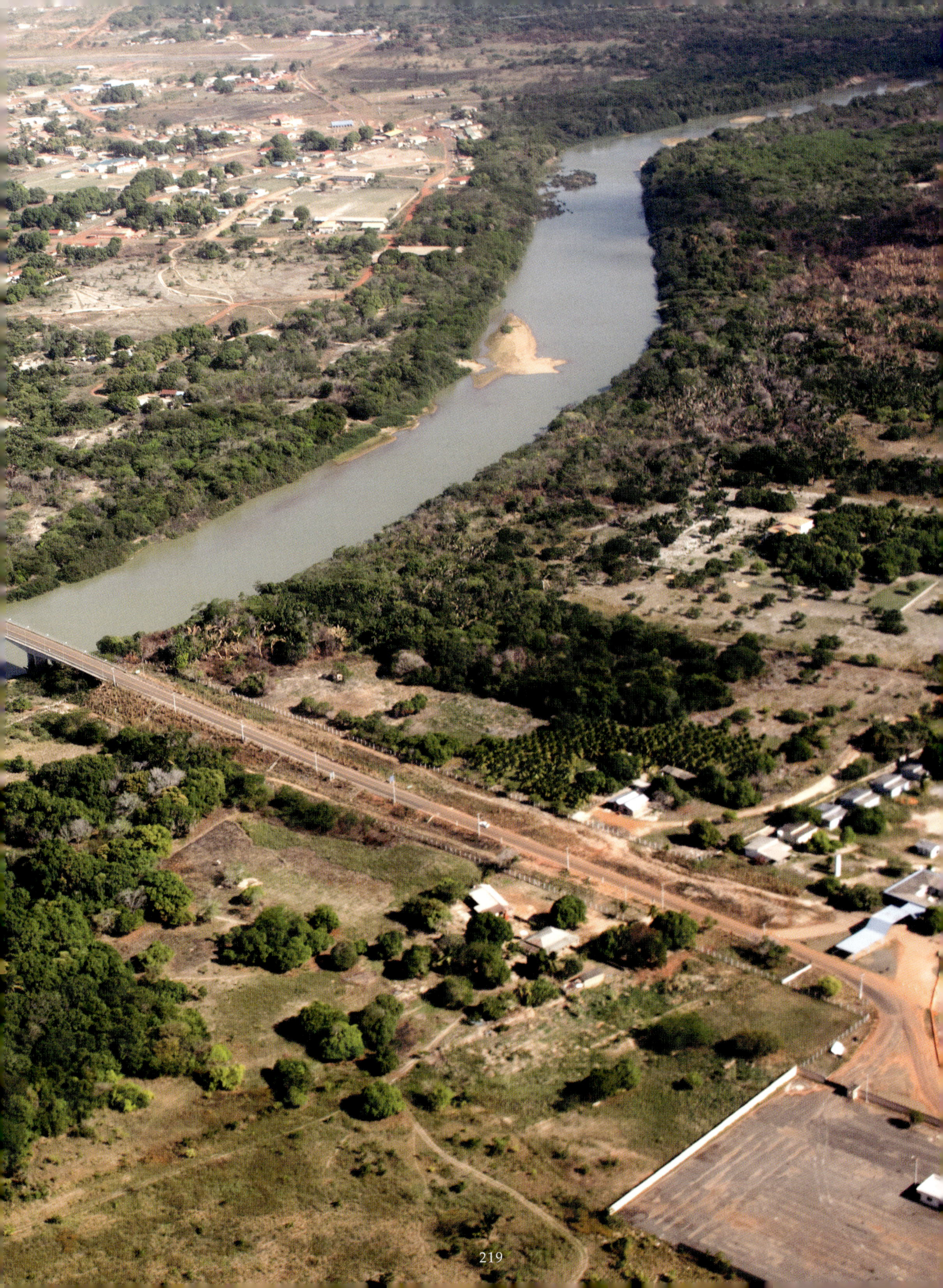

# Guyana from Above

Coastal canal near Abary in Mahaica-Berbice (Region 5) / IB

## Why invest in Guyana?

Geographically, Guyana is in South America; politically and culturally it is part of the Caribbean. The country straddles these two like an Amazonian Colossus offering both investor and visitor a wealth of opportunities and experiences that will reap untold benefits, reveal new vistas and offer up a smorgasbord of delights.

Guyana has declared itself, "open for business" - open to both foreign and domestic investors that include overseas Guyanese.

Why invest? Here's why.

It is a good time to invest in a prime location whose vision is to become the primary investor destination in the region by 2030.

And that vision is boasted by a diversified economy, an array of across-the-board investment incentives, including a flat business tax rate, tax holidays (e.g. 5% royalty on gold mining and full tax holiday on bauxite), waivers of customs duties, export tax allowances and full and unrestricted repatriation of capital, profits and dividends as well as additional incentives in eight priority economic sectors – Agriculture, Tourism, Services, Information and Communications Technology, Light Manufacturing, Energy, Mining and Wood Products.

Furthermore, according to the World Bank 2015 Economic Overview, "The economic output for Guyana is broadly positive. Guyana's growth is projected to remain strong, averaging about 4% per annum".

The government has pledged itself to work to dismantle the bureaucratic barriers and inefficiencies that have characterised trading and investing in the country. Guyana's investment promotion agency, GO-Invest, leads this pledge by providing a 'one stop shop' to investors before, during and after an investment has been realised.

### NATURAL RESOURCES

Endowed with extensive savannahs, productive land and forests, rich mineral deposits of gold, bauxite and diamonds, abundant water resources and an Atlantic coastline, Guyana presents dynamic business

In 2015, French-owned Teleperformance opened a state-of-the art contact centre in the heart of Georgetown. The company provides out-sourcing for customer services, technical support and sales to English-speaking consumers / IB

223

Service engineers from Guyana Telephone and Telegraph Company Limited (GT&T) carry out repairs and maintenance. GT&T is a subsidiary of US telecommunications company Atlantic Tele-Network, which owns 80 per cent of the company. The government of Guyana owns the remaining 20 per cent / IB

Republic Bank (Guyana) Limited was established in 1836 as the British Guiana Bank and was the first commercial bank in the former British colony. As Guyana's first indigenous commercial bank it is also the first bank to be owned by the indigenous private sector. It also has the largest ATM network of all the commercial banks operating in Guyana / IB

opportunities across multiple sectors of its economy.

Whilst recognised globally as a sugar, bauxite and rice producer, the recent discovery of hydrocarbons off the shores of the country is predicted to have a substantial impact on every aspect of the country's economy. The commercial viability of this discovered resource is yet to be determined but expectations are high that massive pre-eminent investment opportunities will be realised.

Guyana's extensive network of rivers and Atlantic coastline also provide ideal conditions for both seafood and aquaculture.

Finally, its pristine environment, unspoiled rainforest and exotic fauna and natural attractions, which include the famous Kaieteur Falls, make Guyana a highly attractive location for eco- and adventure tourism.

LOCATION
Guyana's unique geographic positioning and its socio-political heritage put it at the gateway of South America and the Caribbean. On one hand, its Caribbean and English-speaking heritage enables Guyana to be part of the Caribbean Community (CARICOM), while on the other, it is a South American country, neighbouring two of the most important economies on the continent – Brazil and Venezuela.

DUTY FREE MARKET ACCESS
Through a combination of regional, bilateral and preferential agreements, about 75 per cent of Guyana's exports enter destination markets duty free, with many others receiving duty-reduced access. This is achieved through Guyana's membership of CARICOM, which provides duty-free access to the 15-nation CARICOM market, CARICOM agreements with the Dominican Republic, Colombia, Costa Rica, Cuba and Venezuela, partial scope agreements with Brazil and Venezuela, and bilateral agreements with Argentina, China and Turkey. Guyana also benefits from preferential duty-free or reduced-duty access to major developed country markets through CARIBCAN (Canada), the US Caribbean Trade Partnership and the European Union' (EU) ACP Contonou Agreement.

LANGUAGE
Guyana is the only English-speaking nation in South America. Investors contemplating the installation and operation of service enterprises will find this a distinct advantage. This is especially true for those involved in the growing IT and business process outsourcing (BPO) markets in North America as well as businesses conducting operations to support the activities of large corporations worldwide, and those serving English speaking tourism markets.

AFFORDABLE LABOUR
Guyana has one of the most competitive wage rates when compared to Latin America and the Caribbean. The labour force is well educated with literacy estimated at close to 99 percent and is regarded as trainable and hard working

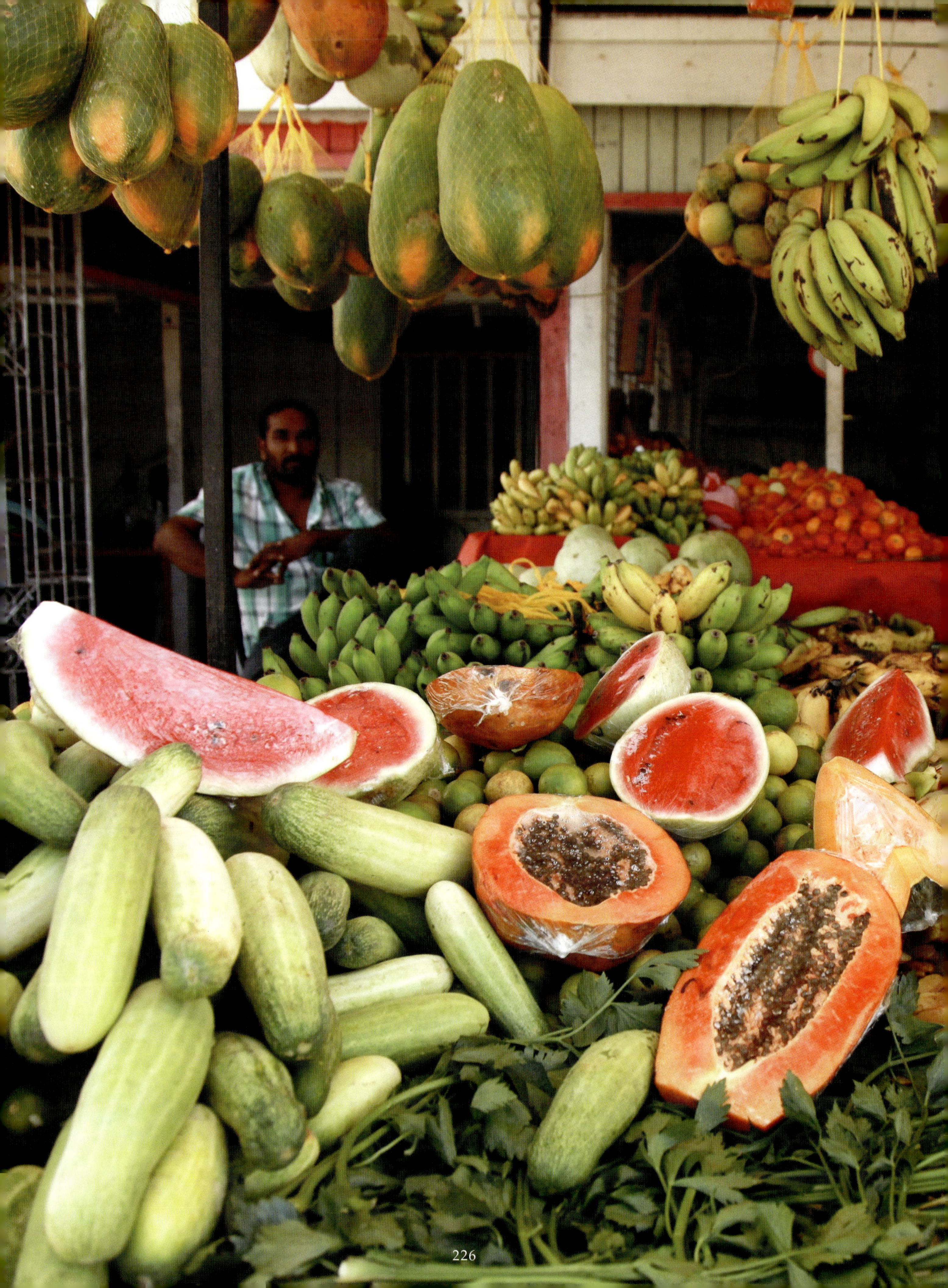

: Fruits and vegetables, both for commercial and subsistence use, are cultivated in all the regions of Guyana / KJ

# Agriculture

Agriculture remains at the very heart of Guyana's people-centred developmental agenda. It is seen as a medium to promote national prosperity, end poverty and hunger and provide the opportunity for better lives for all Guyanese.

The agricultural sector continues to be an important contributor to the Gross Domestic Product (GDP), employment generation, foreign exchange earnings and rural development of the country. Agriculture accounts for approximately 20 per cent of GDP, providing more than 33 per cent direct employment, both at rural and urban levels. The sector comprises five principal sub-sectors: The rice industry; the sugar industry; the non-traditional agricultural commodities (fruits, vegetables, ground provisions, seasoning, etc); livestock including apiculture; and fisheries.

While there are a number of large private and public sector farming enterprises, agriculture is predominantly undertaken by small farmers, farming less than five hectares (ha) of land.

It is estimated that there are 1,740,000 ha of land being used for agricultural purposes, but only about 200,000 ha (500,000 acres) are used effectively with relatively adequate drainage and irrigation. The major contribution comes from rice (90,000 ha), sugar (48,000 ha) and coconut (25,000 ha); non-traditional crops occupy about 30,000 to 40,000 ha and are showing upward trends. About 158,473 ha of agricultural land are used for livestock but it is estimated that about 3.3 million hectares of additional agricultural land can potentially be brought into use. This is an asset that Guyana must begin to use as its economy is developed.

Although Guyana's traditional sugar and rice industries continue to play an important role in the economy, agricultural diversification has been a major pillar in the strategy to broaden the productive base. However, immense opportunities are still unexplored. For instance, while Guyana is self-sufficient in some livestock products – primarily meat – there is minimal export of livestock products.

The fishing industry continues to grow in economic importance and contributes almost 10 per cent to agriculture GDP /IB

The pineapple is one of the most important fruit crops in Guyana / IB

Unloading a plantain harvest at Parika ferry stelling on the Essequibo River / KA

Agro-processing is emerging as an important thrust in agriculture. Outside of sugar, ago-processing targets the production of fresh and unprocessed products. Rice is accelerating its value added production. Currently, the Guyana Marketing Corporation (GMC) is ensuring the operationalisation of Cassava Mill at Parika Agro-Processing Facility.

Water resource management is an important variable in Guyana's agriculture and it is estimated that 94.4 per cent of water withdrawal is for the agriculture sector. The enhancement of the drainage and irrigation system and, in some cases, the sea defences, is the most important challenge the country faces in increased production and productivity in agriculture. In addition, the fishing industry continues to grow in economic importance. It contributes about 9.4 per cent to agriculture GDP; it collects about GY $30.7 million in revenue from fees from licenses and it adds GY $15 billion to the foreign currency earnings through exports of fish. The fishing industry employs around 15,000 people, with approximately 4,000 to 5,600 people directly employed in fishing, with many more benefiting indirectly through fishing related industries. It provides a source of relatively cheap animal protein and is among the highest

Wales Sugar Estate: Although Guyana's traditional sugar and rice industries continue to play an important role in the economy, agricultural diversification has been a major pillar in the strategy to broaden the productive base / IB

per capita consumption of fish and fish products within the Caribbean region. Inland fisheries are now emerging as a more important part of the fishing industry. Guyana has abundant inland aquatic resources and a rich and diverse resource base.

As regulation of trade has increased there are needs for improvements in food safety, agriculture health standards and competitiveness of the produce and products for exports. Guyana, like many other developing countries, is attempting to build effective food safety and agriculture health management systems in the face of multiple deficiencies and limited resources. Enhanced competitiveness through lowering costs of production and reengineering the supply chain for faster time-to-market, is one pillar being pursued.

Over the last fifty years, Guyana's agriculture has primarily been concentrated on the coast; for the next decades, the potential for agricultural development in the hinterland regions will be exploited. In keeping with the 'Year of the Renaissance', the Ministry of Agriculture has been working assiduously for the revitalisation of agriculture in the hinterland. The Government of Guyana's development of the hinterland is a priority with implementation of policies for development of the Intermediate Savannahs and the Rupununi Savannahs. The Intermediate Savannahs have long been considered as the next frontier for agricultural development.

Hinterland development will focus on orchard and nursery development, infrastructure development and rehabilitation, research and innovation, practical skills training for students, enhancement of packaging and labelling of agro-processed products from the hinterland, construction of new weather stations, pasture development, rainwater harvesting and the resuscitation of the rice project for aromatic rice cultivation.

To achieve this, enhanced focus will be placed on the establishment of agriculture stations in the main eco-zones of Guyana, namely, Hosorro (Region 1), Kato (Region 8), Manari (Region 9) and Eibini (Region 10).

Guyana has a competitive advantage in beef production and plans are apace for developing an export market and to also formalise a dairy industry to reduce the country's dependence on milk imports.

It is estimated that there are 1,740,000 hectares of land being used for agricultural purposes / IB

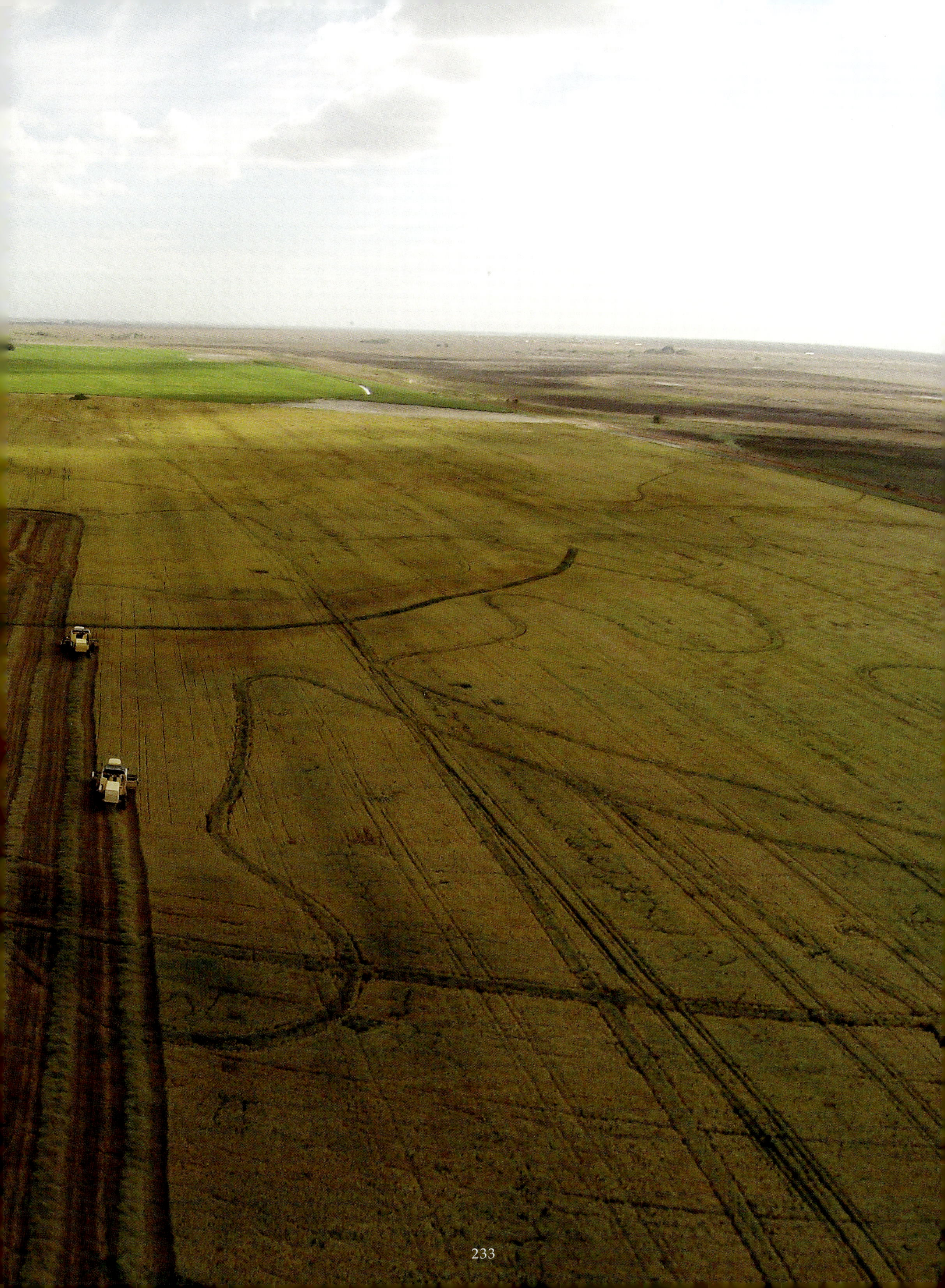

# Caring for the nation's health and well-being

Guyana's health profile has seen significant progress since 1988, consolidated significantly in 2002 with the introduction of a National Health Plan, a comprehensive strategy to provide for the country's healthcare needs. The goal of this plan was the improvement of the spiritual, physical and mental health status of all citizens; health being a state of complete physical, mental and social well-being and not merely the absence of disease or infirmity.

Successive governments have initiated development programmes and strategies to ensure equitable distribution and utilisation of healthcare services, the provision of effective and quality services and generally, the continuing improvement in the health, well-being and quality of life for all Guyanese.

The complex and vast demography of the country poses specific challenges in meeting these goals. Due to this diverse landscape and the sparse distribution of the population, uniform health care delivery to all parts of the country, especially the hinterlands, can be adversely affected but many health care workers now work in the most remote parts of Guyana and all residents are now able to access free, quality health care.

The Ministry of Public Health, through Regional Health Services (RHS), on a regular basis, deploys complete teams of medical personnel into the most remote villages. These teams usually include nurses, specialist doctors (surgeons, paediatricians), laboratory technicians, malaria workers and pharmacists.

Health care staff are the driving force for the delivery of these services. Presently, opportunities exist for the engagement of more highly trained nurses, doctors, midwives, medics, dentists, community health workers, x-ray technicians, medical technologists and other specialists.

Nurses and midwives are the backbone of the health care system in Guyana and nurses can now benefit from the many specialist postgraduate training programs in different medical fields.

Doctors are being trained at the University of Guyana and via bilateral memoranda of understanding (MOUs) through scholarships at various medical schools across the world including Cuba, Russia and China.

The first tier of treatment for any citizen occurs at the country's 166 health posts. These provide preventive and simple curative care for common diseases and attempt to promote proper health practices and are staffed by community health workers. The provision of preventive and rehabilitative care and promotion activities at the next level occurs at 109 health centres, each staffed with a medical extension worker or public health nurse, along with a nursing assistant, a dental nurse and a midwife.

The next tier of treatment is facilitated at nineteen district hospitals which provide basic in-patient and out-patient care and selected diagnostic services. These hospitals are equipped to provide simple radiological and laboratory services, gynaecology and preventive and curative dental care. They are designed to serve geographical areas with populations of 10,000 or more.

Four regional hospitals provide emergency services, routine surgery and obstetrical and gynaecological care, dental services, diagnostic services and specialist services in general medicine and paediatrics. They are designed to include the necessary support for this level of medical service in terms of laboratory and x-ray facilities, pharmacies and dietetic expertise.

The Georgetown Public Hospital Corporation is the highest level of a functioning health service in the country providing a wider range of diagnostic and specialist services, on both an in-patient and out-patient basis. In addition, there is a psychiatric hospital in Canje; a geriatric hospital in Georgetown and one children's rehabilitation centre.

There are also ten hospitals belonging to the private sector and to public corporations, plus diagnostic facilities, clinics and dispensaries in those sectors. Eighteen clinics and dispensaries are owned by the Guyana Sugar Corporation.

Together, these facilities, with the support of trained and committed personnel, are able to strive confidently forward in achieving a better quality of life for, and improvements in the well-being of, all Guyanese.

*Merlin O. Persaud, M.D.*

Georgetown Public Hospital is the country's largest medical facility and has a 600-bed capacity / KJ

Leguan Cottage Hospital serves the Essequibo River islands of Leguan and Wakenaam / KA

Within the last fifty years Guyana has made leaps along with the rest of the world on how information is relayed through media. At the dawn of Independence in 1966, newspaper and radio had been established. Newspapers such as *The Argosy*, *The Creole* and the *Demerara Daily Chronicle* are just three of the many that existed. Radio Demerara and British Guiana Broadcasting Service controlled the airwaves.

Amidst the euphoria of the newly Independent Guyana most newspapers ceased production. By 1973, only the *Guyana Graphic* remained and when the Thompson Group, which owned this newspaper put it up for sale, the then Forbes Burnham-led Peoples National Congress (PNC) Government created laws that allowed them to take ownership of the newspaper. It became the *Guyana Chronicle* and serves as a voice of the state even today.

A few other mainstream newspapers have come into existence since Independence. In 1986, David DeCairies and Miles Fitzpatrick launched the *Stabroek News*. Ten years later in 1996, Glenn Lall set up *Kaieteur News* and in June 2008, Queens Atlantic Investment Inc. launched the *Guyana Times*.

Besides the mainstream dailies many other newspapers have been produced over the last fifty years – religious, cultural, business, entertainment, sports and political newspapers from every part of the country. Political parties have produced newspapers such as *Dayclean*, which belonged to the Working People's Alliance, *Mirror*, the People's Progressive Party and *New Nation*, the People's National Congress.

Today, there are more radio stations than there are newspapers; opposite to what it was in 1966 when the British Guiana Broadcasting Service became Guyana Broadcasting Service. Two years later the Government took control of Guyana Broadcasting Service and it became known as Action Radio. In 1979, Guyana Broadcasting Corporation was established after the Government took control of Radio Demerara and merged it with the Guyana Broadcasting Service.

In 1980, the Guyana Broadcasting Corporation began operating two channels: Channel 1, the general channel, and Channel 2, the regional channel. Sometime later Channel 1 became Radio Roraima and Channel 2 became Voice of Guyana. In 1998, 98.1 Hot FM began broadcasting.

The Guyana Broadcasting Corporation and Guyana Television Broadcasting Limited merged in 2004 to form the National Communications

Spreading the news is both a vocal and visual endeavour / KJ

*Homegrown television broadcast content has burgeoned since the 1990s / KJ*

Network. Until that time the state controlled all radio stations. Change occurred in 2011 when President Jagdeo issued eleven radio licenses. It was criticised as an unlawful act since it is alleged that some of the recipients were closely connected to the President.

Radio stations in operation today include ANG Inc., I Radio Inc., Linden Wireless Communication Inc., Little Rock Radio Station Inc., Freedom Radio Limited, Pinnacle Communication Inc., Radio Guyana Inc., Wireless Connections Inc., NTN Radio and Hits and Jams Entertainment.

Some of these radio stations are linked to television, which began edging into Guyana in 1988. By 1990, Tony Viera had sought the permission of the Government to bring television to Guyana and he established Viera Communications Network. Soon after, Rex McKay established Channel 7. Jacob Rambarran's Channel 13 was soon a part of the line up followed by Channel 6, which was founded by C.N. Sharma in 1992.

At this time the television stations had mostly American content; they did not have licenses. This changed in 2001 when the Government gave out fifteen licenses. The recipients included George Washington Television (GWTV) Channel 2, CNS Inc. Channel 6, Blackman and Sons Inc. (HBTV) Channel 9, Guyana Television Station (GTV) Channel 11, Rambarran Broadcasting System Limited (RBS) Channel 13, STVS Channel 4, Multi Technology Vision Inc. (MTV) Channel 65, NTN Channel 69, MBC Channel 42 & 93, Vision TV Channel 102, all located in Georgetown.

In Berbice, Dave's Television Channel 8 Inc., CCB TV and LRTV Channels 10, 17 and 68 also received licenses along with RCA Television Inc. 8 in Essequibo. Three channels did not apply for licenses at the time: Viera Communications Television Channel 28, WRHM Inc. Channel 7 and 89 and HGPTV – Omar Farouk Inc. Channel 16/67. They felt there were flaws in the system.

Apart from the television stations aforementioned there are others in operation countrywide and many offer a wealth of local news and entertainment. These include Skar Communication Inc. Channel 46, Little Rock Television Inc. Berbice and Flex TV Channel 102. Guyana Learning Channel was set up in 2011 and China Central Television Channel went on air in 2012. State-owned National Communications Network television reaches many regions including Linden, Essequibo and Berbice.

In 2009, Tony Viera sold Viera Communications Television to the Ramroop Group. It now operates under the title Television Guyana Inc. (TVG).

Guyana has certainly shown tremendous growth over the last fifty years where the media is concerned and with the introduction of online news sources such as Demerara Waves, News Source, Inews and Newsnow, the country has secured its place in keeping up with the rest of the world.

---

*Mosa Telford is a dramatist, journalist and winner of the 2013 Guyana Prize for Literature*

# The Guyanese diaspora

The mid-20th century saw the major outflow of migrants from Guyana when a series of push and pull factors influenced the movement of Guyanese to the major urban centres of the United Kingdom and North America.

These factors range from the polarising, internecine violence of the early 1960s, direct recruitment to industries and services, access to professional and tertiary education and training and the impact of legislation that both closed and opened doors.

It is thus no surprise that emigration rates from Guyana is the highest in the world with more than 55 per cent of its citizens residing abroad.

The main outcome of this was the creation of vibrant and striving diasporic communities overseas and Guyana becoming the largest recipient of remittances, relative to GDP, among the whole of Latin America and the Caribbean.

Members of these diasporic communities with an ancestral or parental link to Guyana have made significant contributions to their host societies and to commemorate the 50th anniversary of the nation's independence, it is opportune for these contributions to be recognised, recorded and celebrated.

We acknowledge anyone with a link - residency, parentage or heritage – to Guyana who have achieved public and professional recognition in their chosen career or profession, are iconic role models and exemplars and have pioneered developments illustrative of the Guyanese derring-do character.

There are too many to be named here for the contributions that they have made and are continuing to make to their 'host' and 'home' societies. Though not named here, we salute them.

## THE BRITISH GUYANESE
*by Dr Christopher A. Johnson*

BASED on the re-weighting of the UK's Annual Population Survey, following the results of the 2011 census, the total population of people living in the UK who were born in Guyana was estimated to be in excess of 22,000 with the largest number, 14,000, living in London. Of that number, an estimated 3,000 people retained their Guyanese nationality.

Members of this Guyanese Diaspora have populated every facet of British society, reaching Olympian heights and becoming pioneers, icons and exemplars in all endeavours.

Pioneers who are Guyanese 'Firsts' include Jack London, the first Black athlete to win Olympic gold for Britain; Beryl Gilroy, the first Black primary school head teacher and mother of Professor Paul Gilroy; Dr Samantha Tross, the first Black female orthopaedic surgeon; Lee Woolford-Chivers, the founder of the Nursery Carnival in Notting Hill; Arif Ali, publisher and founder of the nation's longest established Black publishing house, Hansib Publications; Daphne Steel, the first Black matron in a British hospital; Christopher Brasher, the co-founder of the London Marathon and Eric & Jessica Huntley, co-founders of Bogle L'Ouverture Publications and the Walter Rodney Book Shop.

In the literary arts, the British firmament shines bright with several Guyanese luminaries – Edgar Mittelholzer, John Agard, Pauline Melville, Wilson Harris, Grace Nichols, Meiling Jin, Sharon Maas, David Dabydeen, Roy Heath, Michael Abbensetts, Jan Carew, Rupert Roopnarine, Narmala Shewcharan, Peter Kempadoo, Elly Niland, Fred D'Aguiar, Mike Phillips, Marc Matthews and Janice Shinebourne.

In the fields of music and entertainment, the names of Eddy Grant, Leona Lewis, Sol Raye, Phil Lynott, Norman Beaton, Ramjohn Holder, Ken Johnson, Cy Grant, Carmen Munroe, Shakira Baksh, Tommy Eytle, Robert Adams and Rianna Scipio, among many others, are well known.

But it is in the sporting arenas that Guyanese excel with Howard Eastman (boxer), John and Justin Fashanu (football), Narendra Bhairo (power lifter) and the stellar cast of cricketers - Ivan Madray, Glendon Gibbs, Clive Lloyd, Stephen Camacho, Roy Fredericks, Rohan Kanhai, Alvin Kallicharran, Lance Gibbs, Mark and Roger Harper, Colin Croft and Mark Ramprakash. And their exploits with the willow and leather are chronicled to great acclaim by Clem Seecharan.

On the British political landscape, the UK can boast of Sir Shridath Ramphal, Sir Lionel Luckoo, Baroness (Valerie) Amos, Lord (Herman) Ouseley, Lord (Waheed) Alli, Members of Parliament Bernie Grant and David Lammy, and Local Councillors Stephen Padmore and Joe and Kingsley Abrams.

British society also benefited from the interventions of numerous others. The two most prominent activists who rattled the cages of the British establishment were Barrister Rudy Narayan and anti-racism campaigner and Speaker's Corner orator Roy Sawh. Lee Akbar-Samuel was a philanthropic colossus championing social housing, senior citizens and the Caribbean Chinese community, Mark Dalgety is revolutionising the food manufacturing industry with his unique blend of herbal teas and Sybil Phoenix and Yvonne Thompson are the voices of reason campaigning for improvements in the life chances of all Londoners.

There are over fifty Guyanese community organisations looking after the welfare of their members and promoting the culture of the nation, each served by selfless individuals who remain

contributions is impressive as are their numbers, from quiet but sustained interventions by Sindamini Bridglal to the stentorian pleas of educationalist Joy Leach.

## GUYANESE IN THE USA
### by Desmond Roberts

EARNEST migration into the United States began in 1965 with passage of the Hart-Cellar Act which welcomed skilled nationals to New York and Boston; opening immigration doors closed by the 1962 British Immigration Act.

With the collapse of the sugar industry and the Guyanese economy from 1980, nationals sought other opportunities away from the sugar estate and villages to work and live in the Caribbean and the neighbouring countries of Suriname, Venezuela and Brazil. The ongoing migratory haemorrhage drew these migrants further north to Canada and later back south to the USA.

Guyanese of enslaved and indentured origins, except the native Amerindians, were now engaged in their second migration to another alien continent – North America.

Guyanese show the highest proclivity among immigrant groups to remain in New York City. The NYC Department of City Planning identified the 2011 Guyanese NYC population as 139,000. The Migration Policy Institute estimates that in 2014, Guyanese in the USA numbered 273,000. However, it is felt that there are some 350,000 Guyanese in the USA, officially and unofficially, including those first generation identifying as Guyanese.

Guyanese have excelled in the USA, with stars in every field. Academic stars from Ewart Thomas, John Rickford, Ivelaw Griffith and Dennis Benn; sociologists and therapists Kami Roberts, Percy Hinckson, Nathilee Caldeira and Lear Matthews; medical doctors and researchers Rohan Somar, Deborah Persaud, Victor Boodhoo, Donald Culley and wife Carla Crawford and Frank Denbow; dentists Ingram Hazlewood and Eton Wilson; engineers Dr Mewburn Humphrey, Winston Baijnauth, Maya Trotz, Aisha Bryant-Walcott and Colin Westmoreland; public sector administrators Aubrey Featherstone, Bridget Gladwin and Richard Hooper; economist Ramesh Gampat; radio, TV and film luminaries Hugh Hamilton, Kojo Nnmadi, CCH Pounder, Selwyn Collins, Ron Bobb-Semple and Rudy Jadoopat; finance John Butters and Valence Williams; Harvard Law School graduates Ronald Campbell and Denise Grant; cultural promoters Dr Vibert Cambridge, Priya Singh, Claire Goring, Ken Crosbie, Monty Blackmore and Ingrid Griffith; writers Karen Sinclair, Verianne Mentis and Gaiutra Bahadur.

There were Guyanese athletic stars in several sports: Yankees baseball star Mark Teixeira, and Sacramento Kings basketball point guard Darren Collison (son of track stars June and Dennis Collison); boxer Terence Ali; athletes James Wren-Gilkes, Aliann Pompey and Marian Burnett; bodybuilding champions Laura Crevalle and Hugh Ross. There were Guyanese athletes who represented the USA: Jennifer Innis (track) Maritza Correia (swimmer) and table tennis player George Braithwaite.

Guyanese have hundreds of Hometown Associations representing their alma mater churches, villages, former work places and professions. They contribute remittances (World Bank conservative estimate of US$ 280 million or 17% GDP in 2010) to which can be added personal deliveries, gifts and funding for building projects

## GUYANESE IN CANADA
### by Prof Frank Birbalsingh

THE earliest example of a notable Guyanese Canadian is Sir James Douglas (1803-1871), son of a Scottish father and a Guianese mother Martha Ann Telfer. Sir James was the first governor of British Columbia.

Other notable Guyanese-Canadian pioneers include Philip Edwards (1907-1971), an athlete who won five Olympic bronze medals that earned him the nickname 'Man of Bronze' and who represented British Guiana at the first ever Commonwealth Games, held in Hamilton Ontario, in 1930, and at the British Empire Games in London in 1934.

John Rodriguez, a Portuguese-Guyanese migrated to Canada in 1956 where he became an activist in education and politics, joining the National Democratic Party (NDP), Canada's socialist party, and winning seats for the NDP in Federal elections in 1972, 1974 and 1979.

Born in New Amsterdam, Berbice, Ovid L Jackson emigrated to Canada in 1965 and in 1983 became a Member of Parliament for the Liberal Party in the Canadian House of Commons. He was awarded the prestigious Order of Ontario for work related to the needs of young people, newcomers in Canada and people with disabilities.

Post 1970, Guyanese began to distinguish themselves in almost every field of endeavour. Among this whole constellation of stars are entertainers Melanie Fiona, Melinda Shankar, Mark Gomes; literary icons like Cyril Dabydeen (Poet Laureate of Ottawa from 1984 to 1987) Sasenarine Persaud and Andrea Gunraj; and several who excelled in sports - Charles Allen, Troy Amos-Ross, Ian Beckles, Alex Bunbury, Laura Creavalle, Nicholas de Groot, Dwayne De Rosario, Sunil Dhaniram, Philip Edwards, Corinne Van Ryck de Groot, Nicolette Fernandes, Sean Foley, Priscilla Lopes-Schliep, Egerton Marcus, Mark McKoy and Walter Spence.

Others who were recognised for success in their own field of work include Raywat Deonandan (global health), Kazim Bacchus (education), Narine Dat Sookram (radio host), Janice Elizabeth MacGregor (beauty pageant winner), Abdullah Hasan (Guyana Medal of Service), James Yhap (banking) and Aubrey Mille (telecommunications) to name a select few.

## Portuguese (Brazilian)

### GUIANA AOS 50 – REFLEXÃO, CELEBRAÇÃO E INSPIRAÇÃO

A Guiana é o único país da América do Sul onde o inglês é a língua oficial. Conhecida como a "terra de inúmeras águas", é agraciada com uma ampla rede de hidrovias, cataratas e fluentes vertiginosas através de uma vasta faixa de floresta tropical que cobre a maioria dos seus 83.000 metros quadrados. Sua capital é Georgetown.

Delimitada pelo Suriname a leste, pelo Brasil ao sul e pela Venezuela a oeste, suas costas são banhadas ao norte pelo Oceano Atlântico, de onde vêm os ventos alísios que sopram do nordeste. Esta extensão da costa, habitada por mais de 80% da população, em um total de 735.554 habitantes, é considerada um dos mais bonitos e aprazíveis locais para se viver. Situado a 2,13 metros abaixo do nível do mar, o país é protegido, ao longo de sua costa, por uma parede marítima instaurada por holandeses na década de 1880.

Descendentes de indianos representam o maior grupo étnico presente, abrangendo cerca de 44% da população; descendentes de *africanos*, por sua vez, representam cerca de 30%; guianeses pertencentes à herança heterogênea totalizam cerca de 17%; e a população indígena cerca de 9%.

Apesar de o inglês ser considerado sua língua oficial, a maioria da população fala "*Creolese*", uma língua crioula com base inglesa que carrega influências africanas e indianas, variando de acordo com a região do país onde é falada.

O país foi primeiramente colonizado por holandeses no início do século XVII, que buscavam adquirir terras semelhantes àquelas pertencentes às grandes potências europeias. Foi em 1531, entretanto, que os europeus, com a chegada da expedição comandada pelo espanhol Diego de Ordaz, realmente colocaram os pés em solo guianense. A soberania holandesa só foi oficialmente reconhecida com a assinatura do *Tratado de Münster* em 1648.

Os holandeses mantiveram o controle do território ao longo dos 150 anos seguintes. Tanto franceses quanto ingleses, entretanto, tomaram o controle por diversas vezes; foi somente em 1814 que os britânicos decidiram ceder três províncias (Essequibo, Demerara e Berbice).

Nomeado Guiana Britânica em 1831, o país manteve-se sob controle britânico até 1966, quando adquiriu soberania como uma nação independente.

Os primeiros a habitarem as costas guianas foram os indígenas, povo que fora encontrado pelos holandeses quando estes fundaram Essequibo, em 1616. Há, precisamente falando, quatro principais tribos entre os habitantes indígenas: Warraus, Aruaques, Uapixanas e Caraíbas, que incluem, ademais, diversas subtribos, como Arrecunas, Akawaios, Patamonas, Uaiuais e os Macuxis.

Escravos africanos foram trazidos para o país em meados do século XVII. Com a abolição da escravidão e início do *indentureship* (servidão por dívida) em 1835, os portugueses pousaram no país, seguidos por indianos e chineses em 1838 e 1851, respectivamente.

Geograficamente, a Guiana pode ser dividida em cinco zonas amplamente demarcadas: uma estreita planície costeira fértil que avança em direção à plataforma continental, onde reside a maioria da população; uma região acidentada com areia e argila brancas, que contém a maioria das jazidas minerais do país; uma densa floresta tropical localizada na região meridional do país; a *savana* a sudoeste; e uma região montanhosa composta pelas cordilheiras Pacaraima e Kanunu.

A Guiana ostenta a mais larga catarata de queda única do mundo, as Cataratas de Kaieteur, com uma queda de aproximadamente 226 metros, além do mais alto monte do país, o Monte Roraima, de 2.809 metros, situado em sua tríplice fronteira com o Brasil e a Venezuela. Os nomes de suas províncias provêm dos três rios internos do país, Essequibo, Demerara e Berbice. Essequibo é considerado o mais extenso rio do país, com 1.014 quilômetros de extensão, abrangendo 365 ilhas. O Rio Corentyne forma a fronteira com o Suriname.

# Portuguese (Brazilian)

O clima *local* é *tropical* além de ser, geralmente, úmido e quente, apesar de moderado a nordeste devido aos *ventos alísios* ao longo da costa. Há duas estações chuvosas: a primeira ocorre de maio a meados de agosto; a segunda, de meados de novembro a meados de janeiro.

Com a instituição de um sistema regional, o país divide-se, atualmente, em dez regiões.

A Guiana era, tradicionalmente, um país com sua economia voltada à agricultura. Durante o período colonial, essa produtividade foi direcionada quase que exclusivamente à produção açucareira, ainda contribuindo, tanto quanto possível, com 28% para as receitas obtidas pela exportação. Agora abastecida com arroz, bauxito, ouro e diamantes, madeira, pesca e minerais, a economia tem apresentado um crescimento econômico moderado desde 1999, graças à expansão dos setores agropecuário e de mineração, além de uma atmosfera para iniciativas comerciais mais favorável, uma taxa de câmbio mais realista, inflação baixa equitativa e um suporte continuado a organizações internacionais.

Proclamada, em 23 de fevereiro de 1970, como República Cooperativa em sua adesão a uma posição republicana, a Guiana é uma democracia parlamentarista com três poderes governamentais: executivo, legislativo e judiciário. Liderada por um Presidente, integra um sistema de pluripartidarismo, com eleições parlamentares a cada cinco anos. As eleições para o Governo Local são realizadas a cada três anos. Em 11 de maio de 2015, uma coligação pluripartidária multiétnica, a APNU-AFC, ocupou 33 dos 65 assentos na Assembleia Nacional, introduzindo o Brigadeiro (aposentado) David Granger como Presidente.

Em maio de 2016, o país celebrou seu Jubilo de Ouro como uma nação independente, tendo o seu governo atual sustentado a visão de levar o país a novos patamares, fortalecendo seus pontos fortes e, consideravelmente, desenvolvendo e gerenciando seus programas de desenvolvimento em harmonia com o lema da nação: Uma população, uma nação, um destino.

Propósitos de desenvolvimento incluem, ademais, programas de infraestrutura para integração de costas com o interior, a fim de que a Guiana consiga proteger seu território integralmente, além de tornar-se a porta de acesso tanto para o Caribe quanto para a América do Sul de modo a acessar oportunidades de comércio e investimento, diversificando a economia e garantindo que as fontes naturais do país não sejam exploradas no risco de seu patrimônio.

O Ministério de Investimentos e Comércio instaurou medidas de modo a engajar a introdução do Setor Privado, instituir nova legislação para fortalecer o setor comercial, incentivar o empreendedorismo e, através do *Go-Invest* e do Escritório de Investimentos da Guiana, fornecer aos investidores as ferramentas necessárias para incorporar e estruturar sua entrada no mercado local.

A entrada de fornecedores de telecomunicações internacionais proporcionou ao país tecnologia de última geração a fim de otimizar sistemas existentes, como rádio, televisão, telefones fixos e móveis e internet.

O Perfil de Saúde do país alcançou um progresso significativo desde 1988 com a prestação de serviços através de 166 postos de saúde, 109 centros de saúde, 19 Hospitais de Distrito e 4 Hospitais Regionais. Há, ademais, 10 hospitais pertencentes ao setor privado e a corporações públicas, além de instituições de diagnóstico, clínicas e ambulatórios nestes setores. 18 clínicas e ambulatórios são de competência da Corporação de Açúcar da Guiana.

A Guiana, apesar de ser uma nação jovem, é participante ativa no cenário mundial. Com seus programas de desenvolvimento e com seu foco voltado à sustentabilidade e ao impulso da Economia Verde, torna-se o destino preferido por turistas e investidores.

Com suas terras abundantes e diversas fontes hídricas, a Guiana é, exclusivamente, um mundo desconhecido da Amazônia.

## LOS 50 AÑOS DE GUYANA: REFLEXIÓN, CELEBRACIÓN E INSPIRACIÓN

Guyana es el único país de Sudamérica donde el inglés es la lengua oficial. Se la denomina también "tierra de agua" porque la riega una gran red de vías navegables, cascadas y rápidos que fluyen a través de una abundante selva que cubre la mayoría de sus 215 000 km². La capital de Guyana es Georgetown.

Limita al este con Suriname, al sur con Brasil y al oeste con Venezuela, al norte, sus costas están bañadas por el Océano Atlántico desde donde llegan los vientos alisios del noreste. Esta franja costera en la que aún viven más del 80 % de sus 735 554 habitantes es una de las más bellas y cómodas para visitar. A unos dos metros por debajo del nivel del mar, la línea de la costa está protegida en gran parte por un dique construido por los holandeses en los años ochenta.

El grupo étnico más numeroso es de ascendencia india, con un 44 % de la población; los habitantes de ascendencia africana representan un 30 %; aquellos con antepasados mixtos son un 17 % y las poblaciones indígenas representan el 9 %.

Aunque la lengua oficial es el inglés, la gran mayoría de la gente habla "creolese", una lengua criolla basada en el inglés con influencias africanas e indias dependiendo del lugar del país en el que se hable.

El país fue colonizado primero por los holandeses a principios del siglo XVII durante una misión para conquistar tierras del mismo modo que otros grandes poderes europeos. Sin embargo, fue en 1531, con la llegada de una expedición comandada por el español Diego de Ordaz, cuando los europeos pisaron realmente suelo guyanés. La soberanía holandesa fue reconocida oficialmente con la firma del Tratado de Munster en 1648. Durante los siguientes 150 años, los holandeses tuvieron el control del territorio, pero tanto los franceses como los ingleses les arrebataron el poder en diversas ocasiones hasta que finalmente en 1814 las colonias de Esequibo, Demerara y Berbice fueron cedidas a los británicos.

Bajo el nombre de Guayana Británica en 1831, el país estuvo bajo control inglés hasta obtener su soberanía como nación independiente en 1966.

Los primeros en habitar sus costas fueron los indígenas que los holandeses encontraron cuando desembarcaron en Esequibo en 1616. Estrictamente hablando, hay cuatro naciones dentro de los habitantes indígenas: Waraos, Arawak, Wapisiana y Caribes, las cuales incluyen varias sub tribus: Arrecunas, Akawaios, Patamonas, Wai Wai y los Macusi.

Se llevaron esclavos africanos al país a mediados del siglo XVII y con la abolición de la esclavitud y el comienzo de la servidumbre, en 1835, llegaron los portugueses seguidos de los indios en 1838 y los chinos en 1851.

En términos geográficos, Guyana puede dividirse en cinco zonas bien delimitadas: una estrecha y fértil llanura costera que gradualmente se convierte en la plataforma continental donde vive la mayoría de la población; una región accidentada de arena blanca y arcilla donde se encuentran la mayoría de los depósitos minerales de Guyana; la densa selva tropical en la zona sur del país; la sabana al suroeste y la región montañosa compuesta por las sierras de Pakaraima y Kanuku.

Guyana cuenta con la catarata de un solo salto de agua más grande del mundo, las Cataratas Kaieteur, con 226 metros de caída, y la montaña más alta del país, el monte Roraima que se eleva a 2809 metros y se asienta en la triple frontera con Brasil y Venezuela. Los tres ríos interiores de Guyana son el Esequibo, Demerara y Berbice, por los que se dio nombre a sus regiones. El río más largo de Guyana, el Esequibo, alcanza los 1014 km y se dice que contiene unas 365 islas. El río Corentyne conforma la frontera con Suriname. El clima local es tropical y generalmente cálido y húmedo, aunque moderado por los vientos alisios del noreste a lo largo de la costa. Hay

Spanish

dos estaciones de lluvias, la primera entre mayo y mediados de agosto y la segunda entre mediados de noviembre y mediados de enero.

Con el establecimiento de un sistema regional, Guyana se divide actualmente en diez regiones.

Tradicionalmente, la economía de Guyana se basaba en la agricultura. Tras concentrarse durante el periodo colonial casi exclusivamente en la producción de azúcar, esta producción aún representa el 28 % de los ingresos de exportación. Actualmente, su economía está reforzada por el arroz, la bauxita, el oro y los diamantes, la madera, la industria pesquera y la minería y ha demostrado un moderado crecimiento económico desde 1999 gracias a la expansión en los sectores de la agricultura y la minería, un entorno más favorable para las iniciativas empresariales, un tipo de cambio más realista, una inflación realmente baja y el soporte continuo de las organizaciones internacionales.

Proclamada como República Cooperativa en su adhesión al estatus republicano el 23 de febrero de 1970, Guyana es una democracia parlamentaria con tres brazos gubernamentales: ejecutivo, legislativo y judicial. Liderada por un Presidente Ejecutivo, goza de un sistema pluripartidista con elecciones parlamentarias cada cinco años. Las elecciones a los gobiernos locales se celebran cada tres años. El 11 de mayo de 2015, la APNU-AFC, una coalición multipartidista y multiétnica, obtuvo 33 de los 65 escaños en la Asamblea Nacional e invistió al militar (retirado) David Granger como Presidente Ejecutivo.

En mayo de 2016, el país celebra su cincuenta aniversario (Golden Jubilee) como nación soberana y su actual gobierno ha prometido una nueva visión para conducir el país hacia nuevas cotas, construyendo sobre sus fortalezas y desarrollando y gestionando apreciablemente sus programas de desarrollo conforme al lema de la nación: Un pueblo, Una nación, Un destino.

Los objetivos de desarrollo también incluyen programas de infraestructuras para integrar la costa con el interior, para que Guyana pueda proteger su integridad territorial, convertirse en la puerta de acceso para las inversiones y oportunidades de negocio tanto del Caribe como de Sudamérica, diversificar la economía y garantizar que los recursos naturales de la nación no sean explotados poniendo en riesgo su patrimonio.

El Ministerio de Inversión y Negocios ha iniciado algunas medidas para fomentar aún más la entrada del sector privado, establecer una nueva legislación para potenciar el sector empresarial, fomentar el emprendimiento y, a través de Go-Invest, la Oficina de Inversiones de Guyana, ofrecer a los inversores las herramientas necesarias para entender y estructurar su entrada en el mercado local.

La entrada de proveedores de telecomunicaciones internacionales ha aportado las últimas tecnologías para mejorar los sistemas existentes que incluyen la radio, la televisión, la telefonía fija y móvil e Internet.

El perfil sanitario de Guyana ha avanzado significativamente desde 1988 con la oferta de servicios a través de 166 dispensarios de salud, 109 centros sanitarios, 19 hospitales de distrito y 4 hospitales regionales. También hay 10 hospitales que pertenecen al sector privado y a corporaciones públicas, así como instalaciones diagnósticas, clínicas y dispensarios en esos sectores. Dieciocho clínicas y dispensarios son propiedad de la Guyana Sugar Corporation.

Aunque es una nación joven, Guyana es un actor mundial en el panorama global y con estos programas de desarrollo y el enfoque en la sostenibilidad y la promoción de una economía verde, es un destino de primera elección para visitantes e inversores.

Única, con sus abundantes recursos terrestres e hídricos, Guyana es el mundo por descubrir del Amazonas.

# Hindi

## 50 वर्ष का गुयाना- सिंहावलोकन, उत्सव और प्रेरणा

दक्षिण अमेरिका में गुयाना अकेला देश है जिसकी राज भाषा अंग्रेजी है। इसे 'नदियों का देश' कहा जाता है और इसे अपने 83,000 वर्ग मील के अधिकांश भाग पर आच्छादित वर्षा वन की एक विस्तृत पट्टी में से हो कर जलमार्गों, झरनों और नदियों की तीव्र जल धाराओं के एक विशाल नेटवर्क का वरदान मिला है। गुयाना की राजधानी जॉर्जटाउन है।

पूर्व में सूरीनाम, दक्षिण में ब्राज़ील और पश्चिम में वेनेजुएला के साथ इसकी सीमाएँ हैं, उत्तर में इसके समुद्र तट पर अटलांटिक महासागर टकराता है, जहाँ से उत्तरपूर्वी व्यापारिक हवाएँ आती हैं। यह तटीय भूमि जहाँ इसकी 735,554 की आबादी का 80 प्रतिशत अभी भी रहती है, आवास के लिए सबसे सुंदर और आरामदायक स्थानों में से एक है। यह समुद्र तल से कोई सात फुट नीचे स्थित है, जिसकी रक्षा एक समुद्री दीवार करती है जिसका निर्माण 1880 में डच लोगों द्वारा किया गया था।

यहाँ लगभग 44 प्रतिशत भारतीय मूल के लोग रहते हैं जो यहाँ का सबसे बड़ा नस्लीय समूह है; लगभग 30 प्रतिशत लोग अफ्रीकी मूल के हैं; लगभग 17 प्रतिशत मिश्रित विरासत के गुयानावासी और लगभग 9 प्रतिशत यहाँ के मूल निवासी हैं।

जबकि अंग्रेजी राज भाषा है, देश के जिस भाग में बोली जा रही है उसके आधार पर, लोगों की एक बहुत बड़ी संख्या अफ्रीकी और भारतीय प्रभावों वाली, अंग्रेजी पर आधारित 'क्रियोल' भाषा बोलती है।

यूरोप की अन्य महा शक्तियों के समान भू-भाग पर कब्जा करने के लिए सत्रहवीं शताब्दी के आरंभ में डच लोगों द्वारा इस देश को बसाया गया था। हालाँकि, बहुत पहले 1531 में, स्पेनी डिएगो डे ओर्डाज के नेतृत्व में एक अभियान दल के आगमन के साथ ही यूरोपियों के कदम गुयाना की धरती पर पड़ चुके थे। 1648 में मन्स्टर संधि पर हस्ताक्षर के साथ डच प्रभुसत्ता को आधिकारिक रूप से मान्यता मिल गई थी। डच ने अगले लगभग 150 वर्षों तक इस भू-भाग पर अपना नियंत्रण बनाए रखा, लेकिन फ्रांसीसियों और अंग्रेजों दोनों ने कई बार नियंत्रण छीना और अंततः 1814 में एसेक्विबो, डेमेरारा और बरबिस काउंटियाँ अंग्रेजों को सौंप दी गई थीं।

1831 में इसका नाम ब्रिटिश गुयाना रखा गया और यह देश 1966 में एक स्वतंत्र देश के रूप में प्रभुसत्ता प्राप्त करने तक अंग्रेजों के नियंत्रण में ही रहा।

इन तटों पर सबसे पहले बसने वाले यहाँ के मूल लोग थे जिन्हें डच लोगों ने 1616 में एसेक्विबो को बसाते समय यहाँ रहते हुए पाया था। सच पूछिए तो, वहाँ देशी निवासियों के बीच चार प्रमुख राष्ट्र हैं: वराऊ, अरावक, वैप्सियाना और कैरिब जिनमें अनेक उप-जनजातियाँ शामिल हैं: अरेक्युना, अकावाइयो, पटामोना, वाई-वाई और माकुसी।

सत्रहवीं शताब्दी के मध्य में दास बनाए गए अफ्रीकियों को इस देश में लाया गया था, और दास प्रथा समाप्त होने के साथ और 1835 में करारबद्ध सेवा प्रथा के आरंभ में, पुर्तगाली आए, उसके बाद 1838 में भारतीय और 1851 में चीनी आए।

गुयाना को भौगोलिक रूप से, मोटे तौर पर चिह्नित पाँच क्षेत्रों में विभाजित किया जा सकता है: एक संकरा उपजाऊ तटीय मैदान जो क्रमशः एक महाद्वीपीय शेल्फ में परिवर्तित होता है, जहाँ अधिकतर आबादी रहती है; एक पहाड़ी सफेद रेत और मिट्टी का क्षेत्र, जिसमें गुयाना के अधिकतर खनिज भंडार हैं; देश के दक्षिणी भाग में गहन ऊष्ण कटिबंधीय वर्षावन; दक्षिण-पश्चिम में सवाना; और पकाराइमा तथा कनूकू दोनों श्रेणियों वाला पर्वतीय क्षेत्र।

गुयाना में दुनिया का सबसे चौड़ा एकल-बूँद झरना – काएट्योर फॉल्स – है जो 741 फुट की ऊँचाई से गिरता है और ब्राज़ील एवं वेनेजुएला के साथ त्रि-बिंदु सीमा पर स्थित, 9,219 फुट ऊँचा, देश का सबसे ऊँचा पर्वत माउंट रोराइमा है। गुयाना की तीन आंतरिक नदियाँ हैं: एसेक्विबो, डेमेरारा और बेरबिस हैं जिनके नाम पर इसकी काउंटियों के नाम रखे गए थे। गुयाना की सबसे बड़ी नदी एसेक्विबो की

लंबाई 630 मील है और कहा जाता है कि इसमें कोई 365 द्वीप हैं। कोरेंटाइन नदी सूरीनाम के साथ सीमा का काम करती है। स्थानीय जलवायु उष्णकटिबंधीय है और सामान्यतः गर्म तथा आर्द्र रहती है, हालांकि समुद्र तट के साथ-साथ उत्तर-पूर्वी व्यापार हवाएँ इसे मध्यम करती हैं। वर्षा के दो मौसम होते हैं, एक मई से मध्य-अगस्त; दूसरा मध्य-नवंबर से मध्य-जनवरी तक होता है।

क्षेत्रीय प्रणाली की स्थापना के साथ, अब गुयाना में दस क्षेत्र हैं जिन में देश विभाजित है।

पारंपरिक रूप से, गुयाना में एक कृषि-आधारित अर्थ-व्यवस्था थी। औपनिवेशिक काल के दौरान लगभग पूरी तरह से चीनी के उत्पादन पर केंद्रित रहने के कारण, निर्यात से आय में चीनी का हिस्सा 28 प्रतिशत है। अब चावल, बॉक्साइट, स्वर्ण और हीरा, इमारती लकड़ी, मत्स्यपालन और खनिजों से समृद्ध हुई अर्थव्यवस्था में 1999 से मध्यम वृद्धि दिखाई दी है। कृषि एवं खनन क्षेत्रों में विस्तार की बदौलत व्यावसायिक पहलों के लिए एक अधिक अनुकूल वातावरण, एक अधिक वास्तविक विनिमय दर, काफी नीची मुद्रास्फीति दर और अंतरराष्ट्रीय संगठनों का सतत समर्थन संभव हुआ है।

23 फरवरी 1970 को अपनी गणतांत्रिक स्थिति हासिल करने पर एक सहकारी गणराज्य घोषित किया गया गुयाना एक संसदीय लोकतंत्र है जिसमें सरकार की तीन शाखाएँ हैं: कार्यपालिका, विधायिका और न्यायपालिका। एक कार्यपालक राष्ट्रपति की अध्यक्षता में, गुयाना में हर पाँच वर्ष में संसदीय चुनाव की व्यवस्था के साथ एक बहु-दलीय प्रणाली है। स्थानीय सरकारों के चुनाव हर तीन वर्ष में होते हैं। 11 मई 2015 को, एक बहु-नस्लीय, बहु-दलीय गठबंधन, एपीएनयू-एएफसी ने राष्ट्रीय असेम्बली में 65 में से 33 सीटें जीतीं और (सेवानिवृत) ब्रिगेडियर डेविड ग्रैंगर को गुयाना का कार्यपालक राष्ट्रपति बनाया गया।

मई 2016 में, एक प्रभुसत्तापूर्ण राष्ट्र के रूप में देश अपनी स्वर्ण जयंती मना रहा है और इसकी वर्तमान सरकार ने देश को नई ऊँचाइयों तक ले जाने, इसकी शक्ति को बढ़ाने और देश के ध्येय वाक्य: एक लोग, एक राष्ट्र, एक भाग्य के अनुरूप अपने विकास कार्यक्रमों को उल्लेखनीय रूप से विकसित और प्रबंधित करने का वादा किया है।

विकास लक्ष्यों में तटीय भूमि को आंतरिक इलाकों के साथ एकीकृत करने के लिए संरचनात्मक कार्यक्रम भी शामिल हैं, ताकि गुयाना अपना क्षेत्रीय अखंडता की रक्षा कर सके, कैरीबियन और दक्षिण अमेरिकी दोनों के लिए निवेश एवं व्यापार अवसरों का उपयोग करने के लिए एक प्रवेश द्वार बन सके, अर्थव्यवस्था में विविधता ला सके और सुनिश्चित कर सके कि देश की विरासत के जोखिम पर उसके प्राकृतिक संसाधनों का दोहन नहीं किया जाता हो।

निवेश एवं व्यापार मंत्रालय ने निजी क्षेत्र के इनपुट का दृढ़ता से समावेश करने, व्यापार सेक्टर को सुदृढ़ करने के लिए नए कानून बनाने, उद्यमिता को प्रोत्साहित करने और निवेश के लिए गुयाना कार्यालय, गो-इनवेस्ट के माध्यम से स्थानीय बाजार में अपने प्रवेश को समझने और संरचित करने के लिए निवेशकों को आवश्यक साधन प्रदान करने कई उपाय आरंभ किए हैं।

अंतरराष्ट्रीय दूरसंचार सेवा प्रदाताओं के प्रवेश से रेडियो, टेलीविजन, फिक्स्ड एवं मोबाइल टेलीफोन और इंटरनेट सहित मौजूदा प्रणालियों के संवर्धन के लिए नवीनतम प्रौद्योगिकी आई है।

गुयाना ने स्वास्थ्य के क्षेत्र में, 166 स्वास्थ्य पोस्ट, 109 स्वास्थ्य केंद्रों, 19 जिला अस्पतालों और 4 क्षेत्रीय अस्पतालों के माध्यम से सेवाएँ प्रदान कर के 1988 से उल्लेखनीय प्रगति की है। उन क्षेत्रों में निजी क्षेत्र और सार्वजनिक निगमों से संबंधित 10 अस्पताल, नैदानिक सुविधाएँ, क्लिनिक और डिस्पेंसरियाँ भी हैं। गुयाना चीनी निगम के स्वामित्व वाले अठारह क्लिनिक और डिस्पेंसरियाँ हैं।

हालांकि गुयाना एक युवा देश है, वैश्विक पटल पर यह एक वैश्विक शक्ति है और इन विकास कार्यक्रमों तथा एक हरित अर्थव्यवस्था की वहनीयता पर ध्यान केंद्रित करने और प्रोत्साहन के साथ यह आगंतुकों और निवेशकों के लिए गंतव्य की पहली पसंद है।

अद्वितीय रूप से, अपने स्थल और जल संसाधनों की प्रचुरता के साथ, गुयाना अमेजन का एक अनदेखा संसार है।

# Chinese (Mandarin)

**圭亚那建国 50 周年 – 反思、庆祝和鼓舞**

在南美洲,圭亚那是唯一以英语为官方语言的国家,首都位于乔治城。它被誉为"多水之乡",纵横交错的水道、瀑布和湍流,穿越大片热带雨林,其面积占据 83,000 平方英里土地的大部分地区。

圭亚那东邻苏里南,南临巴西,西接委内瑞拉,北濒大西洋,从那里吹来东北信风。国内人口有 735,554 人,其中 80% 依然生活在海滨,这里堪称世界上最美丽舒适的栖居地之一。在海岸线海平面下大约七英尺处,有荷兰人于 1880 年代修筑的防波堤,保护着大部分海岸。

印第安后裔是这里最大的民族,约占人口的 44%,非洲裔约占 30%,混血圭亚那人约占 17%,原住民约占 9%。

尽管英语是官方语言,但大部分人说克里奥尔语 (Creolese),这是以英语为基础,带有印第安和非洲语言影响的混合语言,具体取决于在国家的哪个地区使用。

17 世纪初,这个国家首先被荷兰人殖民,他们意在谋求获得类似欧洲其他大国的土地。但在 1531 年,西班牙人 Diego de Ordaz 率领探险队来到这里时,其实是欧洲人第一次踏上圭亚那这片土地。1648 年,明斯特条约(Treaty of Munster)的签订,标志着荷兰统治权正式得到认可。随后 150 年左右,荷兰人掌控着这片领地,但法国和英国都在不同时期试图夺取控制权。最终,英国在 1814 年让埃塞奎博 (Essequibo)、德梅拉拉 (Demerara) 和博比斯 (Berbice) 三个郡臣服归顺。

1831 年,这个国家被命名为英属圭亚那,直到 1966 年作为独立国家取得主权之前,它一直处于英国控制之下。

这片海岸的第一批定居者,是荷兰人于 1616 年入驻埃塞奎博 (Essequibo) 时发现的土著居民。严格来讲,土著居民有四个主要民族:瓦瑙斯 (Warraus)、阿拉瓦卡斯 (Arawaks)、瓦皮西亚纳斯 (Wapisianas) 和卡里布斯 (Caribs),其包括几个更小的部落、阿雷库那斯 (Arrecunas)、阿卡瓦伊奥斯 (Akawaios)、帕塔莫纳斯 (Patamonas)、瓦伊-瓦伊斯 (Wai-Wais) 和马库西斯 (Macusis)。

17 世纪中叶,非洲奴隶被带到圭亚那。随着 1835 年废除奴隶制和开始服务契约期,葡萄牙人来到这里。随后印度人和中国人分别于 1838 年和 1851 年陆续前来。

在地理上,圭亚那可被分为五个广阔的分区:狭长肥沃的海岸平原,逐渐延伸到大陆架,这里聚集着数量最多的人口;白沙和黏土丘陵区域,拥有圭亚那的大部分矿藏;国家南部密集的热带雨林;西南部的大草原;以及山区,包括帕卡伊马 (Pakaraima) 和卡努库 (Kanuku) 山脉。

圭亚那拥有世界上最宽的单条瀑布 – 凯厄图尔瀑布 (Kaieteur Falls) – 垂落 741 英尺,该国的最高峰罗赖马山 (Mount Roraima) 高达 9,219 英尺,矗立在与巴西、委内瑞拉相接的三国交界点上。圭亚那的三条内陆河是埃塞奎博河 (Essequibo)、

### Chinese (Mandarin)

德梅拉拉河 (Demerara) 和博比斯河 (Berbice)，它的三个郡也由此得名。圭亚那最长的河流埃塞奎博河 (Essequibo) 长达 630 英里，据称其中有 365 座岛屿。科伦提内河 (Corentyne River) 形成与苏里南的边界。

当地气候是热带气候，通常很湿热，但沿着海岸的信风让气候变得柔和一些。一年有两个雨季，第一个从 5 月到 8 月中旬，第二个从 11 月中旬到 1 月中旬。

随着区域体系的建立，圭亚那现在被分为十个地区。

圭亚那传统上是一个农业国。在殖民时期，该国基本上只从事食糖生产。如今，食糖依然占据着国家出口收入的 28%。现在受到大米、铝土矿、黄金和钻石、木材、渔业以及矿产的支撑，经济自 1999 年起出现适度增长，这要归功于农业和采矿业的扩张、更有利的商业发展氛围、更切实的汇率、相当低的通胀以及国际组织的持续支持。

1970 年 2 月 23 日建立共和政体时，圭亚那就宣告自己为合作共和国，采取议会民主制，拥有行政、立法和司法三套政府机构。由行政总统担任元首，施行多党制，每五年进行一次议会选举。地方政府每三年举行一次选举。2015 年 5 月 11 日，多民族、多党联盟 APNU-AFC 赢得国民大会 65 个席位中的 33 个，任命 David Granger 准将（已退休）担任行政总统。

2016 年 5 月，圭亚那庆祝成为主权国家 50 周年，现任政府承诺以国家实力为基础，大力发展和管理恪守国训 —"一个民族、一个国家、一种命运"— 的发展计划，将该国提升到新的高度。

发展目标还包括融合沿海地区与内陆地区的基础设施计划，这样圭亚那就能保护其领土完整，成为加勒比和南美洲的门户，以抓住投资和贸易机遇，实现经济多元化，并确保在利用国家的自然资源时不会让这些遗产面临风险。

投资和商业部推出了各项措施，以更坚定地利用私营领域的力量、实施新法律以强化商业、鼓励创业，并通过圭亚那投资署 (Go-Invest) 为投资者提供了解并规划进入地方市场的必要工具。

国际电信服务提供商的进入，带来了尖端技术，增强了包括广播、电视、固定和移动电话以及互联网在内的现有系统。

自 1988 年起，圭亚那通过 166 处卫生站、109 个健康中心、19 家地区医院和 4 家地区医院，让国民健康状况得到极大提升。此外，还有属于私营和股份有限公司的 10 家医院，以及这些领域的诊断设施、诊所和药房。圭亚那糖业有限公司 (Guyana Sugar Corporation) 拥有 18 家诊所和药房。

尽管圭亚那还是个年轻的国家，但它已经登上全球舞台。有了这些发展计划，加上注重可持续发展和促进绿色经济，它必然成为游客和投资者的首选之地。

圭亚那还拥有独一无二的丰富土地和水资源，是亚马逊地区尚未开发的一片乐土。